EARLY EAST TEXAS

A HISTORY FROM INDIAN SETTLEMENTS TO STATEHOOD

Joe Ellis Ericson

HERITAGE BOOKS
2008

HERITAGE BOOKS
AN IMPRINT OF HERITAGE BOOKS, INC.

Books, CDs, and more—Worldwide

For our listing of thousands of titles see our website at
www.HeritageBooks.com

Published 2008 by
HERITAGE BOOKS, INC.
Publishing Division
100 Railroad Ave. #104
Westminster, Maryland 21157

Copyright © 2002 Joe Ellis Ericson

Other books by the author:

The Nacogdoches Story: An Informal History

They Came to East Texas, 500-1850: Immigrants and Immigration Patterns
Joe E. Ericson and Carolyn R. Ericson

All rights reserved. No part of this book may be reproduced or transmitted in any form or by any means, electronic or mechanical, including photocopying, recording or by any information storage and retrieval system without written permission from the author, except for the inclusion of brief quotations in a review.

International Standard Book Numbers
Paperbound: 978-0-7884-2187-7
Clothbound: 978-0-7884-7482-8

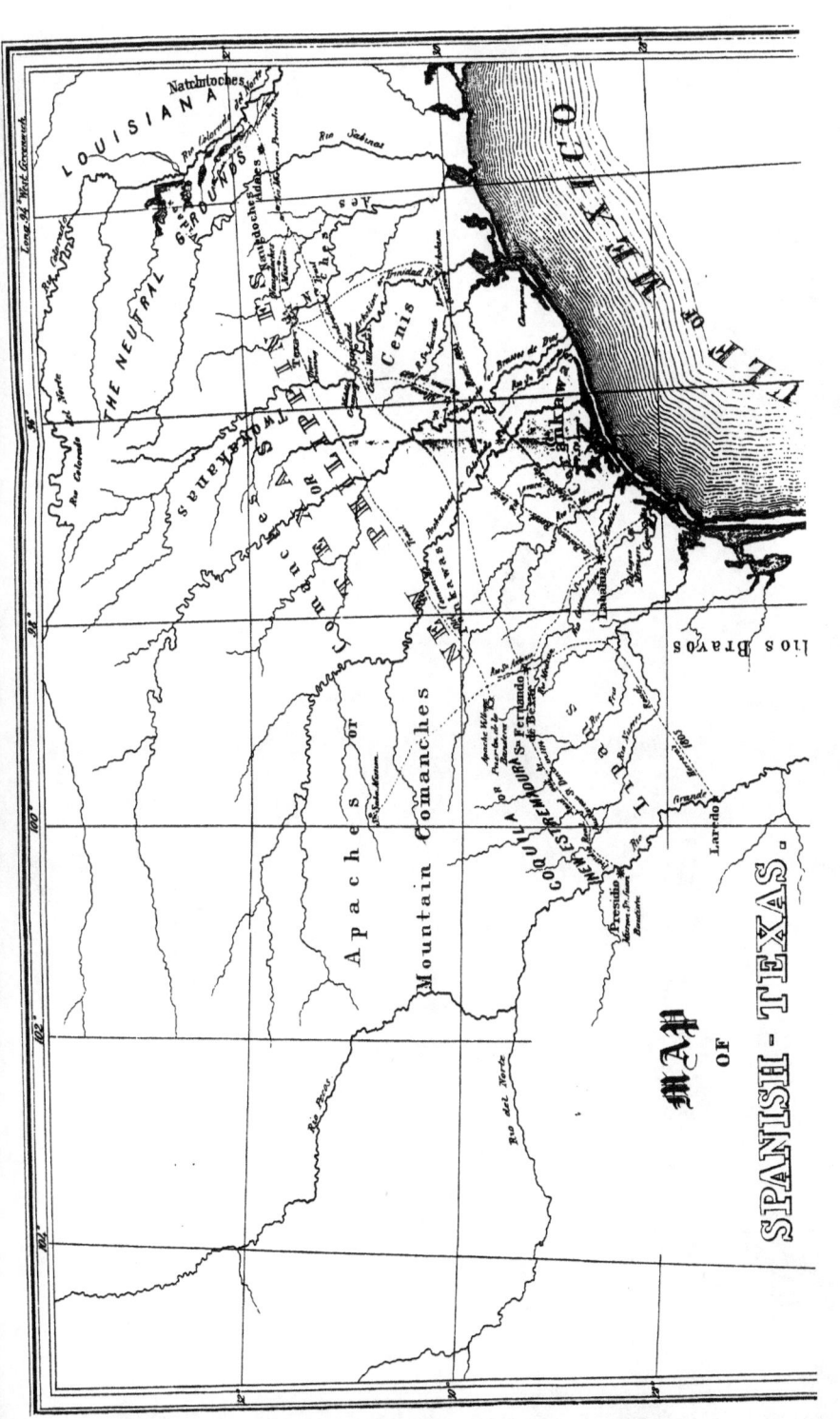

TABLE OF CONTENTS

PREFACE 1
PROLOGUE 3
CHAPTER ONE: EARLY SETTLEMENTS . . 7
    The Europeans Arrive 9
    Founding Permanent Settlements 21
CHAPTER TWO: FILIBUSTERING YEARS 39
    Philip Nolan 39
    Magee-Gutierrez Expedition 46
    The Long Expedition 57
CHAPTER THREE: THE FREDONIAN REBELLION 65
    Antecedents: The Reentry 67
    An Empresario Comes 75
    A Rebellion Launched 87
CHAPTER FOUR: TRANQUIL YEARS 91
    The Redlands 92
    Civil Government for San Augustine . . 97
    The Municipality of Nacogdoches . . 100
    The Town of San Augustine 104
CHAPTER FIVE: THE BATTLE OF NACOGDOCHES 109
    The Battle Erupts 110
    Elsewhere in East Texas 116
CHAPTER SIX: REVOLUTION/AFTER . . 123
    Conventions in 1832 and 1833 126
    Consultation of 1835 and Convention of 1836 132
    Revolutionary Days in East Texas . . . 144
CHAPTER SEVEN: EVENTS IN THE LIFE OF THE REPUBLIC 151

    The Cordovan Rebellion 153
    The Cherokee War 158
    The Regulator-Moderator Feud 162
    Local Affairs 169
CHAPTER EIGHT: EDUCATION AND
    RELIGION 177
    Education in East Texas 178
    East Texas Religion 192
CHAPTER NINE: LAW AND JUSTICE ... 213
    Complex Legal System 213
    Legal Practice and Practioners 222
    Courts and Judges 225
CHAPTER TEN: PHYSICIANS AND
    MEDICINES 239
    Physicians 240
    Medical Practice 246
CHAPTER ELEVEN: LIFESTYLES 249
    Amusements 250
    Architecture and Daily Life 256
EPILOGUE 272
APPENDICIES 281
    Appendix I East Texas Congress: Republic of Texas 283
    Appendix II District and County Judges: Republic of Texas 293
    Appendix III East Texas Bar 295
    Appendix IV East Texas Delegates: Convention of 1836 297
    Appendix V East Texas Physicians .. 298
BIBLIOGRAPHY 301
INDEX 305

PREFACE

This history of the people and places in the early history of East Texas was written to put them in the setting of the history of Texas in the years leading up to statehood. Focusing on the four Mexican Municipalities of Nacogdoches, San Augustine, Sabine, and Shelby (Tenaha), it draws on the extensive research done by a variety of historians and local authors in the time since 1932 when the Reverend George L. Crocket's <u>Two Centuries in East Texas</u> was published.

Crocket's seminal work as well as the records of the people of East Texas accumulated and published by Carolyn Reeves Ericson in 1987 and 1991 under the title <u>Nacogdoches: Gateway to Texas</u> and William R. Hogan's <u>The Texas Republic: A Social and Economic History</u> furnish the basis for much of the information about the people's lives and their lifestyles. Other general and local histories and works dealing with special events and activities are identified in the bibliography. The text is fully indexed, but items in the appendices are not included in the index.

Footnotes are utilized to help identify the persons and places mention in the body of the text and sources are identified in a bibliography that includes all of the works utilized. A series of appendices provides the names and on occasion other information

EARLY EAST TEXAS

of some of the leading men who stamped their personalities on the region. This history is intended to be a companion volume to a study of the personalities of the East Texas frontier published by Ericson Books of Nacogdoches in 1998.

Acknowledgment is due Carolyn R. Ericson and Linda Ericson Devereaux for their editorial work in preparing this history. All errors, however, are the responsibility of the author not the editors.

EARLY EAST TEXAS

PROLOGUE

The history of East Texas as a site for European and Anglo American colonization began in the region between the Neches River on the west and the Sabine River on the east and centered on the town of Nacogdoches and San Augustine. It was also bounded on the north by Cherokee Indian bands located in the present Texas counties of Smith, Cherokee, Rusk, and Van Zandt and on the south by the Angelina River. It included part or all of today's Nacogdoches, San Augustine, Sabine, and Shelby Counties.

Colonization of the Nacogdoches District as a permanent Spanish settlement began in earnest between 1779 and 1800, while the Ayish Bayou District in San Augustine County emerged as a permanent Anglo American colony between 1824 and 1835. East of the East Texas settlements were the French outposts in Western Louisiana, while in and around them were the villages of the Caddo Indians, and west of them the vast distances along the Royal Road to San Antonio de Bexar.

After the termination of the American Revolution, Anglo American explorers and other adventurers began to cross the Sabine in a number of places and push their way into the interior of Texas. They were as time proved but the forerunners of the

EARLY EAST TEXAS

march of Anglo American immigrants across the continent. Moreover, a number of American Royalists (Tories) unwilling to face the unpleasantness of continued residence in the American states emigrated to Texas seeking a more desirable place of residence.

By the early years of the Nineteenth Century a sizeable number of foreigners were settled in today's Nacogdoches, San Augustine, and Sabine Counties. Some of them were Irishmen from Louisiana, including John Quinalty, and American traders, among whom were Edmund (Raymundo) Quirk, Henry Quirk, Edward Murphy, William Barr, and Samuel Davenport. Many of these men married Spanish women and quickly assimilated.

Little information as to the origin and background of most of these men has come down to the present. Most, if not all, of them became bona fide settlers, cleared fields, planted crops, built homes, raised horses, raced the horses they bred, and planted themselves permanently in the soil of East Texas.

The communities of Nacogdoches and San Augustine were unique separated generally by the Attoyac River; Nacogdoches predominantly Spanish Catholic and San Augustine predominately Anglo American Protestant. Each in its own way grew up in the wilderness almost entirely ignored and unsupported, developing by the sheer force of the native vigor and resolution of its residents. Both were

EARLY EAST TEXAS

practically disowned by the countries from which they came, and found little welcome from any man in the land to which they had immigrated. In time they became the interior gateway to the United States for commerce and immigration and a buffer against the Cherokee Indians to their north.

Here a singular set of events combined to turn these communities into a "seedbed" for a revolution that would separate the Province of Texas from Spanish-Mexican control and ultimately add it to the union of American States.

EARLY EAST TEXAS

CHAPTER ONE

EARLY SETTLEMENTS

As the Eighteenth Century reached its midpoint, the region now known as East Texas was a virgin forest of pine and hardwood trees. Interspersed here and there along with creeks and rivers were villages of Caddo Indians who had occupied the area for more than a thousand years. These communities consisted of a varying number of small units frequently strung out for as much as twenty miles along the valley stream.

They normally contained a ceremonial center with earthen platform mounds that were utilized for temples and special political events. Present day Nacogdoches was the site of one of these centers. Its location at the confluence of two flowing streams now identified as La Nana and Banita Creeks between two low hills provided an ideal setting.

The East Texas Caddos lived a sedentary lifestyle in peaceful horticultural societies. They cultivated and harvested corn, beans, squash, pumpkins, tobacco, and sunflowers in small garden plots in the fertile soil along the watercourses. They also tended orchards of peaches, plums, figs, and chestnut trees. Both men and women worked the gardens and orchards; and on occasion the men hunted deer, fish, and small game. When convenient they also hunted bison for a food source and for their hides which were used for bedding and clothing.

Caddos engaged in much cooperative endeavor helping each other erect houses and plant crops. Their ceremonial centers, the focal points of their societies, contained their temples and the houses of their principal political and religious leaders. Their houses were large and substantial. Many were as much as fifty feet in diameter. They were constructed by setting posts in the ground vertically to form a circle with a wall some five feet in height. A high conical roof consisting of a framework of rafters and cross beams lashed together and covered with overlapping bundles of grass forming shingles was then erected over the wall. The finished product was a house some twenty to thirty feet high with a spacious interior.

These sedentary Indian bands venerated fire and kept a perpetual fire burning in their temples situated on the earthen mounds they had laboriously created. They engaged in some unusual customs. For example, they welcomed travelers and other strangers who entered their villages with loud and prolonged wailing by all members of the community. In addition these visitors were greeted with elaborate feasts, entertainments, and a variety of gifts.

EARLY EAST TEXAS

As the century began drawing to its close, their centuries-old existence began to undergo a dramatic change. From Frenchman entering their territory from the north down the Mississippi from Canada and from the south upriver from their base at New Orleans and from Spanish penetration from the south and west from their bases in Mexico and the Caribbean, Europeans commenced their inexorable onslaught.

The Europeans Arrive

Learning of the settlement of a French colony in East Texas led by Robert Cavalier, Sieur de La Salle, in 1685, Spanish officials in Mexico City determined to locate and destroy the French post. On the fourth attempt to discover the settlement, in 1689 a Spanish expedition led by the governor of Coahuila found it in ruins and its inhabitants dead or dispersed. Soon after he reported to the Spanish Viceroy in Mexico City, the Count of Galvez authorized an expedition to found a mission among the Tejas Indians in the region. He was convinced that it was necessary to occupy the province of Texas in order to prevent further intrusion by any foreign power.

The expedition set out in March 1690 amidst news that war had broken out between Spain and France and rumors of other Frenchmen living among the Indians. The enterprise had a decidedly military appearance as 110 Spanish soldiers accompanied the four Catholic priests who were to establish the first mission in East Texas. On May 22 they reached the site of a Tejas village which they named San Francisco de los Tejas where they set about to construct the necessary mission structures. This spot was probably on San Pedro Creek to the northwest of present day Weches in Houston County.

The expedition's leaders recommended the establishment of a line of four forts between Coahuila and the land of the Tejas Indians with missionaries stationed at each fort. This action, they believed, would safeguard communications between San Francisco de los Tejas and bases in Coahuila, prevent further foreign trespass, and insure the peaceful conversions of the Indians to the Catholic faith. The Viceroy, instead, approved the recommendations of Catholic officials for the creation of seven additional missions without military along with them.

Thus, in 1691, the Governor of Texas and Father Massanet organized yet another expedition to East Texas. A military escort of fifty soldiers accompanied the missionaries, and after traveling three months they reached San Francisco de los Tejas in August. On arrival Massanet learned that a second mission, Santisimo Nombre de Maria, had been established on the banks of the Neches River further to the east. He also discovered that an epidemic had killed one of the priests and many of the Indians in the vicinity. The Indians, now disillusioned and convinced that the baptismal waters had caused the sickness, had grown sulky and impudent, refused to attend services, and stolen the mission's horses and mules.

Inadequate supplies prevented the creation of the proposed missions and the bulk of the expedition's forces returned to Coahuila. Only Father Massanet and two other missionaries remained under the guard of nine soldiers. A relief expedition was ordered and a pack train of supplies dispatched. They arrived in June 1693 but Massanet and his companions had already determined to abandon the mission.

Santisimo Nombre de Maria had been destroyed by flood waters, new epidemics had broken out in the area causing the death of many Indians and another of the priests, the mission crops had been lost to flood waters and drought. The Indians grew even more hostile, refused to be baptized, stole the mission livestock, and threatened the lives of the missionaries. Massanet's position became so desperate that he packed what could be carried, buried the mission bells and cannon, set fire to the buildings, and departed for Coahuila.

After some three years of activity, lack of proper support from Spanish officials brought about the failure of the first Spanish attempt to occupy East

EARLY EAST TEXAS

Texas. But these first efforts to establish European settlements in East Texas had not been altogether without lasting impact. The Spaniards had gained valuable knowledge concerning the geography and Indian inhabitants of the region, and their initial failures had demonstrated that missions without accompanying presidios and settlements could not succeed.

Early in the Eighteenth Century France became entangled in European wars and an expedition under the direction of Pierre Le Moyne, Sieur d'Iberville was deflected to Biloxi by Spanish vigilance. With the danger of French intrusion temporarily at bey, officials of New Spain lost interest in the Tejas Indians and occupation of East Texas.

In 1714, however, Louis Juchereau de St. Denis, French commander at Biloxi, reached the Rio Grande and there contacted Spanish officials seeking permission to establish trade relations with the Indians in East Texas and Spanish settlements elsewhere in Mexican territory. After learning of St. Denis' activity, officials in Mexico City determined to renew efforts to establish a series of missions in eastern Texas and to take the necessary steps to hold that land against any attempt at French occupation.

Thereafter, in 1716, an expedition commanded by Captain Domingo Ramón set out from San Juan Bautista. It came to consist of seventy-five persons, including soldiers and priests. In June the party crossed the Brazos River and met with a hunting party of Tejas Indians. Indian leaders were invited to a meeting at the Spanish camp near the Neches River where the Spaniards gave assurances of good will.

A few days later, missionaries selected a site for their mission. They chose a location several leagues further east. Father Hidalgo was placed in charge of this reestablished mission, and it was named Nuestra Padre Señor San Francisco de los Tejas. Captain Ramón then led his party across the Angelina River at a site later known as Goodman Bridge, and after traveling only a short distance they came upon the principal Hasinai (Caddo) village where a second mission, Nuestra Señora de la Purisma Concepcíon de los Hainai, was established. Father Gabriel Vergara was left in charge. Moreover, Ramón established a presidio nearby to protect these two missions. The fort, Presidio Nuestra Señora de los Dolores de los Tejas, was situated on a hill just west of Mill Creek in southwestern Nacogdoches County three miles west of the town of Nacogdoches.

The Spanish commander then led his party about nine leagues east-southeast of Mission Conception to the Nacogdoches village at the site of the present day City of Nacogdoches. There he founded a third mission, Nuestra Señora de Guadalupe de los Nacogdoches. In early July a

EARLY EAST TEXAS

temporary log church and dwelling houses for the missionaries was erected and Father Antonio Margil de Jesús placed in charge. The mission's buildings stood on a slight rise overlooking Banita Creek.

Ramón next led the expedition to the northwestern part of today's Nacogdoches County where he selected a site for a mission among the Nazoni and Nadaco Caddos. This mission was located on Dill Creek near the county line of present day Rusk County, about ten leagues west-northwest of the Nacogdoches mission and about seven leagues northwest of Mission Concepcíon. It was named Nuestra Señor San Jose de los Nazonis and Father Benito Sanchez placed in charge.

During the fall months Ramón established two more missions: San Miguel de Linares de los Adaes on the Arroyo Hondo near present day Robeline, Louisiana, and Nuestra Señora de los Delores de los Ais, about one-half mile south of present day San Augustine, Texas. With these missions in place, Captain Ramón completed his assignment and firmly established Spanish ownership by occupation of the territory.

In 1718, Don Martin de Alarcón, Governor of Texas, visited the new East Texas missions. After completing his inspection and bringing about some reorganization of affairs, the Governor returned to San Antonio de Bexar without bolstering the missions

EARLY EAST TEXAS

with settlers, more soldiers, and help in congregating the Indians.

The precarious situation of the missions grew worse in 1719 when war erupted anew between Spain and France. The French inhabitants of Louisiana resented the Spanish occupation of eastern Texas, seeing it as a hindrance to French expansion and a threat of Spanish attempts to expand their settlements beyond the Arroyo Hondo in present day western Louisiana. Using the war as a justification for their actions, French forces led by the commander at Natchitoches attempted to drive the small contingent of missionaries and soldiers out of East Texas. A lay brother resident at Los Adaes fled and delivered the news of the French action. The Spanish settlers, soldiers, and missionaries quickly retreated first to Mission Concepcion, then to Mission San Francisco, and ultimately to the Trinity River. Finally, in despair when no help came from San Antonio, they abandoned East Texas altogether and traveled further west to the Texas capital.

The next year, a Spanish expedition under the command of the Marquez of San Miguel de Aguayo, governor of Coahuila, Texas, and the New Philippines, was dispatched the reestablish Spanish control over East Texas. The Governor was ordered to reoccupy the Province of Texas, restore the priests to their missions, and establish a military post among the

EARLY EAST TEXAS

Caddos. Aguayo's contingent was made up of 500 soldiers, 600 head of cattle, 900 sheep, 800 mules burdened with supplies, and 4,000 horses as mounts for the soldiers.

In July 1721 the Spanish commander met with St. Denis, the French commander, at the site of Mission Concepcion where the Frenchman agreed to return with his forces to Natchitoches. Aguayo then crossed the Neches River and reestablished the mission at the Neches village and renamed it San Francisco de los Neches. Thereafter he oversaw the restoration of Mission La Purisima Concepcion. After a round of ceremonies the Spanish commander assured the Indian tribes of East Texas that they would never again be abandoned and that Spanish soldiers would protect them.

Under his direction Mission San José de los Nazonis, Mission Nuestra Señora de Guadalupe de los Nacogdoches, Mission Nuestra Señora de los Dolores de los Ais, and Mission San Miguel de Linares de los Adaes were restored. In addition, a hexagonal-shaped presidio with a stockade of pointed logs was constructed nearby and named Nuestra Señora del Pilar.

These restored missions in East Texas were agencies of the Spanish monarchy as well as the Catholic Church. Their task was not only to Christianize the Indians of the region but also to

EARLY EAST TEXAS

extend, civilize, and maintain the frontier for their King. By 1731, Spanish claims to the territory had been firmly established, but missions and presidios together were proven unable to prevent further French intrusions into Spanish territory.

Meanwhile, General Pedro de Rivera had been dispatched to the area in 1724 to determined the true state of affairs. He finally arrived in East Texas in early 1727. The general reported to his superiors that forts were poorly constructed, accompanied by grass-roofed houses, garrisons understaffed by soldiers with little notion of military discipline, the manual of arms, or their martial duties. Guard duty was performed irregularly and sentinels rarely posted.

Rivera ultimately recommended the abolition of the Presidio Dolores de los Tejas, and the Viceroy readily approved. The governor of Texas was instructed to notify the presidio's captain and garrison. Their salaries were to be paid through June 1729, but they were discharged and not allowed to reenlist.

The mission priests became very concerned that they were to left without military protection. They petitioned the Viceroy requesting that the presidio be reestablished and the garrison at Los Adaes strengthened. Without the military to keep order, they feared the Indians, armed with French guns and gunpowder, would become thieves. If the Viceroy was determined to carry out Rivera's recommendations,

EARLY EAST TEXAS

they asked to be allowed to relocate their missions or abandon Texas. A portion of them ultimately relocated to sites along the San Antonio River.

Despite the unsettled conditions that still persisted in East Texas, by 1731, Spanish claims to Texas had been established and its boundaries drawn and acknowledged. The province was considered a buffer zone administered as a part of the Kingdom of New Spain, subject directly to the Viceroy and Audencia at Mexico City in civil and military areas and to the Archbishop of Guadalajara in religious matters.

The capital of the province was situated at its easternmost outpost, Los Adaes, only fifteen miles west of the Red River and the French outpost at Natchitoches. The three missions remaining in East Texas were San Miguel de Linares de los Adaes near present day Robeline, Louisiana; Nuestra Señora de Guadalupe de los Nacogdoches on the site of the present City of Nacogdoches; and Nuestra Señora de los Ais situated about half way between these two near present day San Augustine, Texas.

Although trade with the French in Louisiana was forbidden by royal decree, Los Adaes and the surrounding area was so far removed from the nearest sources of Spanish supply that they depended heavily on Natchitoches for much of their food supply and other essentials. The very existence, therefore, of the

EARLY EAST TEXAS

Spanish settlements was dependent upon the French, the very people against whom they were expected to protect the eastern frontier of Spanish Texas.

Conditions at Los Adaes continued to deteriorate, so that by the winter of 1734, the walls of stockade were rotting down, its cannons no longer in place, and large portions of its earthworks washed away by rain. The soldiers were forced to wear dirty blankets or buffalo robes while out of doors, their women and children were forced to remain inside their huts for lack of clothing. They were also without soap, often sick, and reduced to eating poor food.

Circumstances under which the missionaries labored were little better. They faced epidemics of measles, smallpox, and colds; were without enough soldiers to congregate the Indians at the mission pueblos, and supplies remained insufficient to care for neophytes long enough to complete their conversion to Christianity. The Indians, moreover, were able to obtain food from the French as well as trade goods and thus preferred the French to the Spanish.

Distances also plagued the missionaries. The lone missionary stationed at Nacogdoches was compelled to minister to Caddo villages that ranged about ten leagues north and south. After 1749 he had to travel some twenty leagues to minister to the tribe. Still later had to visit other bands of Indians some ten to twenty leagues to the west, and fourteen leagues to

EARLY EAST TEXAS

the northwest.

On an inspection trip in 1767-1768, Father Gaspar Jose de Solis found the mission at Nacogdoches situated on a small plain overlooking the Banita Creek. The shingle-roofed adobe church and the wooden house of the missionaries were both clean but showing some signs of decay. Its wooden stockade included within it a kitchen, a granary, the soldiers' quarters, and other small buildings.

Cession of the Louisiana Territory to Spain in 1763 at the end of the French and Indian War eased the threat of French encroachment that had prompted the Spanish to establish the East Texas missions and presidios. With Spain in possession of Louisiana, Spanish colonial officials no long felt compelled to maintain expensive outposts on the eastern frontier of Texas. The result was a decision in 1773 to completely abandon the forts and missions.

A royal decree issued in 1772 commanded that the presidio at Los Adaes be dismantled and settlers in the vicinity moved to San Antonio de Bexar. The missions at Nacogdoches, Los Ais, and Los Adaes should be abandoned, officers and men discharged, and allowances of the missionaries discontinued. Persons in their vicinity were also commanded to remove to San Antonio.

The Los Adaes people left their homes in early June, although some resisted by fleeing to

EARLY EAST TEXAS

Natchitoches while others hid among the Indians. After traveling some thirty leagues (seventy-eight miles), they reached the ranch called El Lobanillo owned by Antonio Gil Y'Barbo. There they paused to rest and some twenty-four persons were left to follow later.

By the end of July the marchers had reached Nacogdoches where nine others were left and where three were left in their graves. There Y'Barbo assumed command and led the refugees on to San Antonio where they arrived in late September, three months after being forced to leave their homes.

Founding Permanent Settlements

One man, Antonio Gil Y'Barbo was destined to become the "Father of Nacogdoches" and thus the spearhead of permanent European settlement in East Texas. He was a native of Spanish Texas having been born about 1729 at Los Adaes, then the provincial capital of Texas. His father, Matheo Antonio Y'Barbo, was a soldier stationed at Los Adaes, and his mother, Juana Luzgarda Hernandez, was the daughter of a long-time resident of the presidio of San Antonio de Valero. Both parents were almost certainly natives of the province of Andalusia in the Spanish Kingdom. As a child Gil Y'Barbo able to take advantage of all available opportunities for an education, as good as could be expected at a frontier post. He acquired a good command of the Spanish language and an education that combined formal subjects with practical frontier skills.

Los Adaes had been settled in 1721 by thirty-one families, but by 1773 the Spanish frontier post had grown to more than 500 inhabitants. Their homesteads were generally located along the Royal Road from Los Adaes to Nacogdoches. Young Gil grew to manhood in this thriving settlement where he acquired considerable knowledge concerning trading among the French settlers of Louisiana, the Spanish settlers of Texas, and Caddo Indians throughout the region. This knowledge would permit him to be a successful trader throughout the remainder of his life.

Following his marriage to Maria Davila Padilla, Gil Y'Barbo took up land on the Royal Road just west of the Sabine River on Lobanillo Creek where he established a ranch known as Rancho Lobanillo. It was located not far from the Spanish mission at Los Ais, near the modern city of San Augustine, Texas. Y'Barbo could not obtain legal title to his ranch because it was situated within twenty leagues (about 52.5 miles) of the eastern border where Spanish colonial regulations prohibited permanent settlement.

For some years, Y'Barbo divided his time between Los Adaes and his Rancho Lobanillo and engaged in a thriving smuggling trade among the French, Spanish, Americans, and Indians. Although such trade was expressly prohibited by colonial regulations, it was accepted as normal practice by East Texas colonists. As a result of his land holdings and trading enterprises, by 1772 he had become one of the most influential and affluent men on the eastern Spanish frontier.

During these years he trafficked in horses and furs which were collected throughout Central Texas, brought through the Nacogdoches areas, smuggled into French Natchitoches, and shipped down river to New Orleans. About 1770, Hugo O'conor, Spanish commandant Inspector of Presidios, reported to his superiors that Y'Barbo had once been imprisoned for complicity in smuggling horses and mules into Louisiana. Nevertheless, Y'Barbo was empowered to purchase supplies for the presidio at Los Adaes on behalf of the Spanish government.

Gil Y'barbo's peaceful and prosperous existence as a frontier trader and rancher came to an end in 1773 as a result of terms included in the Treaty of Paris that terminated the Seven Years' War. He, along with other Spanish residents of East Texas were forced to remove bag and baggage to San Antonio de Bexar.

Shortly after their arrival at the San Antonio River, the displaced East Texans were informed by

EARLY EAST TEXAS

Governor Ripperda that they could select any vacant lands within the jurisdiction of the village of San Fernando for their new homes, fields, and pastures provided they did not interfere with those already settled there nor the Indians in the area of the mission.

In addition, they were informed that they would have to bear the cost of building irrigation ditches, flumes, and other aids to cultivation. Inasmuch as most of the East Texans were without funds, they could not comply leaving them without any practical means by which they could support themselves or their families. The refugees consequently promptly refused to choose lands or accept any offered them.

Above all else, they wished to return to their homes in the East Texas forests. Not surprisingly, eight days after their arrival, their leader Gil Y'Barbo called a meeting of the heads of families who drafted a petition addressed to royal authorities in Mexico City pleading for permission to retrace their steps and regain their homesteads. Governor Ripperda advised them to carry their petition to the Viceroy, Antonio Bucarelli. Y'Barbo and Gil Flores were chosen to deliver the petition along with a letter of recommendation from Ripperda. The Viceroy denied permission to return to East Texas, but instead permitted them to locate eastward in "a suitable place."

EARLY EAST TEXAS

With the Viceroy's permission in hand, the Spanish governor designated a site on the right bank of the Trinity River known as Paso Tomas situated at the crossing of the Royal Road and the La Bahia (Goliad) Road above the mouth of Bidais Creek in present day Madison County. In keeping with these instructions, refugees selected Gil Y' Barbo as their captain, Gil Flores as their lieutenant, and Juan de la Mora as their alferez (sub-lieutenant) and made preparation to depart.

They left San Antonio in August 1774 and reach the site on the Trinity River in February 1775 where they began construction on wooden houses, corrals, fields, roads and an improved river crossing. The new settlement was name Bucarelli, and an official census revealed a total of 347 inhabitants.

Life went along reasonably well in the little settlement on the banks of the Trinity for nearly four years. But in 1779 a combination of events featuring a series of Comanche Indian raids and a Trinity River flood prompted a number of the families, including Y'Barbo's own family, to begin leaving the settlement. In the midst of this exodus a fire swept through the post destroying half of the houses and damaging others. Taking advantage of the opportunity thus presented, Captain Y'Barbo and Lieutenant Flores determined to lead the exiles back to East Texas without waiting for official sanction.

EARLY EAST TEXAS

Captain Y'Barbo merely informed the provincial governor at San Antonio of the intention of the group and started to the east along the Royal Road and home. The governor responded, not with official censure, but with Y'Barbo's appointment as Captain of Militia and Lieutenant Governor of Nacogdoches and an annual salary of 500 pesos. Failure of the attempt to resettle the East Texas colonials first at San Antonio and later at Bucarelli was largely the result of the reality that they were the descendants of generations of Spanish settlers who had put down roots in Eastern Texas and Western Louisiana and because their leader had both courage and tenacity.

During the early spring days of March or April 1779, Y'Barbo led his 300 to 350 road-weary band of settlers into the little valley between the La Nana and the Banita Creeks later to be known as Nuestra Señora del Pilar de Nacogdoches. In returning his fellow East Texans to their homes Y'Barbo had almost single-handedly brought about the negation of an order of His Most Catholic Majesty, the King of Spain. When his group of settlers occupied the Nacogdoches site, a new epoch in the history of Spanish settlement of East Texas began with its center at Nacogdoches rather than at Los Adaes. The period of permanent European occupation of the region had begun.

Captain Y'Barbo's request to be allowed to establish a commissary or trading post at

EARLY EAST TEXAS

Nacogdoches to accommodate trade with the local Indians was soon granted, and he quickly became the most influential Spaniard of the day among the Indians. Almost certainly, he erected the Stone House (later to become known as Old Stone Fort) in 1779 to accommodate this new trading venture, and it served as its headquarters for many years.

In spite of his reputation as a trader who engaged in illegal smuggling activities, Y'Barbo was made Lieutenant Governor and Militia Captain because colonial officials at San Antonio and Mexico City recognized that he was probably the only man who could hold the colonists together, deal successfully with the local Indian tribes, and maintain satisfactory relations with the French and the Americans to the east.

Soon after their arrival at Nacogdoches, Captain Y'Barbo urged the returned exiles to construct homes for themselves. Using available materials, they placed sharpened tree trunks in the ground to form palisades in a square or rectangular pattern, strengthened them with interlaced vines, and covered all with red mud for insulation. Hipped roofs of shingles extending well beyond the wall protected them from rain and other elements. A stick and mud chimney in one wall provided warmth, illumination, and a place to cook the family's food.

By 1780, Y'Barbo could report to his superiors

EARLY EAST TEXAS

in San Antonio that the settlement at Nacogdoches numbered 400 inhabitants, including fifteen Negro slaves. The number grew to 480 by 1790 and to some 600 by 1800. At that time, the little East Texas post had grown up around a town square known as the Plaza Principal with Y'Barbo's Stone Fort and store on the square on at its northeast corner.

The Old San Antonio Road (El Camino Real)[1] ran through the Plaza Principal connecting the French settlement called Natchitoches in nearby Western Louisiana with San Antonio and the Spanish colonial settlements along the Rio Bravo (Rio Grande). Visitors to Nacogdoches recalled that on special occasions, residents of the community walked around the square speaking an assortment of languages and wearing clothing designating a variety of ethnic

---

[1] El Camino Real, King's Highway, Old San Antonio Road, San Antonio-Nacogdoches Road. Considerable portions of this route from Mexico to Louisiana probably existed long before the Spanish arrived. Some of the segments were a series of Indian trails that linked one native village to another between Natchitoches, San Augustine, Nacogdoches, San Antonio, and locations along the Rio Grande. The distance from the Rio Bravo (Rio Grande) and the Sabine River was approximately 550 miles.

backgrounds. By 1800 Nacogdoches had become the second largest Spanish settlement in Texas.

From 1779 to 1791 or 1792, Gil Y'Barbo had governed the settlement with total authority. He laid out the town in blocks and streets following the traditional Spanish pattern of plazas around the military, religious, government, and other centers. Prior to 1779 the mission priests and the garrison of soldiers had provided law and order. Y'Barbo saw the need for a more formal arrangement, promulgating a strict code of civil and criminal regulations.

The steady growth in population brought with it demands for land. Those seeking title to the lands they settled on appealed to Lieutenant Governor Y'Barbo to provide them with legal titles. In the absence of any formal legal machinery for granting titles to land, from 1779 to 1792 Y'Barbo developed his own informal methods of making verbal grants, and in this fashion disposed of vast estates at will. Although his method satisfied the settlers in and around Nacogdoches, they alarmed and disturbed the orderly legal mind of the provincial governor.

As a consequence, in 1792 the governor sent an inspector to look into Y'Barbo's land dealings. The inspector promptly censured the Lieutenant Governor for granting land illegally, on at least one occasion 50,000 acres in one grant. No official records of such land transactions were made causing the inspector to post a proclamation requiring those persons without written legal grants to their lands to petition the colonial government for titles. The result of all this activity was to obscure land titles and create squabbles over ownership that persisted for decades thereafter.

By 1800, the thriving settlement at Nacogdoches demonstrated what permanent settlers who were allowed even encouraged to move into the fertile forest regions of Eastern Texas could do toward a successful colonization of the province. Its people also demonstrated that contact between them and the Caddo and other Indian tribes of the area could be accomplished peacefully.

A Spanish census conducted in 1788 numbered between 200 and 250 Spanish and French residents of the Nacogdoches district housed in some eighty or ninety wooden buildings. Just over a decade later, the population had increased to some 500 persons, and an extensive commerce with Louisiana was in place. The 1791 Census had shown that number was composed of 172 adult males, 123 adult females, ninety-eight boys, ninety-three girls, and eighteen slaves.

Y'Barbo's term as the governing agent in Nacogdoches came to and end in 1791 when he tendered his resignation in the face of continuing accusations that he persisted in engaging in smuggling contraband goods into Nacogdoches and trading with the Indians for horses stolen from the Spanish settlers. Although an investigation cleared Y'Barbo of all charges brought against him, he was forbidden to return to Nacogdoches from San Antonio.

While the Spanish colonists were creating a permanent European settlement around Nacogdoches, Europeans and Anglo Americans began to infiltrate the East Texas region. They came in despite the existence of a military garrison located at Nacogdoches that was expected to guard against and expel an intrusion by foreigners. Initially most of them were traders eager to participate in commerce with the local Indians, notwithstanding the fact that the Spanish government had reserved to itself a monopoly over trade with its colonies. Spanish colonial regulations declared that all commerce must be handled through accredited agents of the government. No private traders were permitted to deal with Indians without a license.

An examination of Spanish records for the period after the American Revolution demonstrates that English and Irish immigrants from New England and Virginia had begun moving into the Nacogdoches District. In addition, Spain had adopted a policy of encouraging immigration from Ireland near the end of the Eighteenth Century, and some of these settlers drifted into East Texas. An enumeration of foreign nationals living in the Nacogdoches District about

EARLY EAST TEXAS

1804 contains some fifty names.

Indeed, a description of Nacogdoches in the last decade of the century maintained that the town presented a busy aspect, its narrow streets lined with wooden buildings diverging in all directions from Y'Barbo's Stone House. On fiesta and other gala days, the town would be filled with farmers and stock raisers mingling with the townspeople; with Indians of several tribes with their furs seeking out the American traders; French and Spanish visitors; and a random officer in his uniform or a Catholic priest in his robe.

The town's residents were characterized as "simple hearted, busy, and contented." They were happy in their secluded pastoral life, optimistically believing that they would one day be able to obtain legal titles to their homes. They planted, tilled, and harvested crops they produced from their simple, rude agricultural practices. They found that melons and beans would grow with little cultivation. Corn could be harvested in seasonable years, and tobacco could be raised in selected patches. Most also planted and gathered the produce of a garden.

About 1800 into this colony of Spanish settlers a small group of Anglo Americans most of whom were enterprising traders or exiles fleeing from the world to hide themselves in the wilderness arrived. They were the vanguard of the hundreds, even thousands, of immigrants that would soon pass

EARLY EAST TEXAS

through this "Gateway to Texas."

By far the most enterprising and successful trading enterprise in Nacogdoches during the period of Spanish colonization was that of Barr and Davenport. In 1798, William Barr, Luther Smith, Edward Murphy, and Samuel Davenport entered into a partnership to operate a trading firm in Nacogdoches under the name of Barr and Davenport. Two years later Barr secured from Spanish colonial officials a monopoly for the new firm over trade with all Indian bands in Texas. At the same time Davenport was designated the local agent for the enterprise, and he, in due time, established his headquarters in the Old Stone House on the town square in Nacogdoches.

Senior partner William Barr was a native of Londonderry, Ulster County, Ireland born there around 1762 who had immigrated to Philadelphia Pennsylvania just prior to the American Revolution. As he grew older he moved to Pittsburgh, served in the United States Army as a captain for three years, and about 1786 immigrated to Louisiana. The following year he became a naturalized Spanish citizen while he was presumably engaged in the mercantile business in Natchitoches. In 1793, he moved further west to Nacogdoches were he continued in the mercantile business. Barr died in Nacogdoches, and in his will left three-fourths of his estate to his partner Samuel Davenport.

EARLY EAST TEXAS

Another partner, Edward Murphy, was also born in Ireland in the town of Navare. About the time of the American Revolution he also immigrated to Pennsylvania and ultimately by 1786 to Spanish Louisiana. The third partner, Luther Smith, had earlier in life been a resident of New York, but by early in the Nineteenth Century he too was residing in Louisiana.

The remaining partner, Samuel Davenport, was born in Carlisle, Cumberland County, Pennsylvania in 1764. Little is now known of his early life, but surviving records do reveal that he went to frontier Mississippi with his family around 1785. From there he soon went further west to French Louisiana. About 1794 his mother and father both died, Samuel determined to immigrate to Spanish Texas, arriving in Nacogdoches later that same year. During those years he was employed by several well known mercantile firms before branching out on his own account.

For more than a decade (1798-1812) the House of Barr and Davenport was the premier trading company in East Texas and the Neutral Ground of Western Louisiana[2]. At that time settlers, most

---

[2] The Neutral Ground (Territory) was created by a treaty between the United States and Spain in 1806. It provided that the Spanish would remain west of the Sabine

without official permission, moved into the area. Many of them were traders, filibusterers, and slaves. They used the Neutral Ground, a long and narrow strip of land lying between Louisiana and Texas, whose ownership was disputed for some fifteen years by Spain and the United States, as a bridge leading them into Spanish Texas.

Although Spanish colonial regulations placed tight restrictions on and at other times prohibited commercial dealings between Louisiana and Texas, urgent necessity for supplies that developed frequently compelled frontier authorities on both sides of the disputed territory to ignore or amend the regulations when prudence and need dictated. The firm of Barr and Davenport however, was authorized to freight merchandise across the Neutral Ground from Louisiana to Texas and transport furs and livestock back to Louisiana.

The firm was permitted to engage in trade across the international boundary because Spanish authorities recognized the necessity of supplying Spanish troops in East Texas and securing presents to distribute to the Indians to cement their loyalty to the Spanish crown. It prospered in these early years of the

---

River and the Americans east of the Arroyo Hondo, thus creating a "No Man's Land" where no government ruled.

EARLY EAST TEXAS

Nineteenth Century, when in addition to its normal business of supplying the friendly Indians of the area with articles of merchandise it also furnished the Spanish quartermaster's department in Nacogdoches with flour, beef, salt, soap, and chili to supplement similar articles furnished from bases in San Antonio.

The firm kept trains of oxcarts and mules constantly plodding between Natchitoches and Nacogdoches loaded with tobacco, lead, gunpowder, beads, vermillion, flints, axes, hoes, knives, combs, awls, scissors, wire, sugar, blankets, handkerchiefs, and clothing materials. They were reimbursed in cash by the Spanish and in horses and furs by the Indians.

Trade with the Indians was not without risk, however, as it often resulted in bad debts, and their trains of merchandise were occasionally seized by American soldiers on charges of smuggling. Moreover, there were persistent attacks on their trains by freebooters and other lawless elements that inhabited the Neutral Ground.

By 1810 Davenport was the only surviving partner of the firm, and although the partnership had been dissolved by the death of then other three, he continued to operate the business until 1812. During the time he managed the firm through shrewd business acumen and inheritances, Davenport amassed a considerable personal fortune and became one of community's acknowledged leaders.

EARLY EAST TEXAS

Davenport and other residents of East Texas in the early years of the century did not dream that political upheavals and revolutions in both Europe and America were to produce echoes that would disturb their peaceful existence. Even though France had transferred ownership of the Louisiana Territory to Spain in 1762, in 1800 the insatiable French Emperor Napoleon Bonaparte, compensating Spain with territory elsewhere reestablished French control. He intended to develop it into a source of food for the French West Indies ending their dependence on the United States.

Military failures in the Indies and at New Orleans coupled with President Thomas Jefferson's determination to rid the region of French occupation led in 1803 to the Louisiana Purchase whereby the United States acquired title to this hugh undefined territory. This land acquisition placed the land hungry Anglo Americans on the eastern boundary of Texas just across the Sabine River.

In addition, when the French Emperor conquered Spain in 1808 and placed his brother on its throne, the Spanish colonies in America were unwilling to transfer their allegiance to their new Bonaparte king. A revolt soon erupted in Mexico, and although it was ultimately crushed civil war continued at intervals until 1821 when Mexico secured its independence.

EARLY EAST TEXAS

In the midst of the resulting confusion, Americans with dreams of empire and financial gain who became known as filibusterers began crossing the Sabine River and harassing the Province of Texas. From 1785 to 1820, these intruders added yet more disarray to political and economic conditions in the province.

EARLY EAST TEXAS

CHAPTER TWO

FILIBUSTERING YEARS

With the acquisition of the Louisiana Territory by the United States in the early years of the Nineteenth Century, Spanish authorities repeatedly expressed their fear that the Anglo Americans thus poised on their colonial Texas frontier were filled with expansionist political designs. Traders from Louisiana had illegally appropriated much of the Indian trade in the area and offered a ready market for horses stolen from the residents of their frontier outposts. Many of them openly defied the authority of Spanish officials and the requirements of Spanish colonial regulations. The most famous of these defiant traders was Philip Nolan.

Philip Nolan

Many historians have regarded Philip Nolan as the first of a series of filibusterers who infiltrated Spanish-held East Texas in the first two decades of the Eighteenth Century. On the other hand, a Twentieth Century biography maintains that instead Nolan was merely a horse catcher motivated by personal profit.

EARLY EAST TEXAS

In any case, early Nacogdoches records indicate that he was born in Belfast, Ireland in 1771 and that he had settled in Kentucky by 1788 when he became bookkeeper and shipping clerk for General James Wilkinson. From that year until 1791 Nolan represented the general in business transactions in New Orleans where he learned of the rich opportunities for trade in the nearby Spanish province of Texas.

That same year Wilkinson helped Nolan obtain a passport to visit Texas on a trading expedition. While in the Spanish territory, Nolan was viewed with suspicion by local authorities and his goods were confiscated. His association with the infamous American general caused also early Texas historians to view his activities in Texas as political in character.

For the next two years he lived among the Comanche and other northern tribes above the Spanish settlements and then returned to New Orleans with fifty mustangs and a number of animal skins. Nolan was back in Nacogdoches in mid-year 1794 with yet another passport permitting him to secure horses for a Louisiana mounted regiment. While there he pursued confidential inquiries concerning introduction of trade goods for Texas Indians. He believed that the Provincial Governor gave him confidential assurance that his projected trading

EARLY EAST TEXAS

activities would be acceptable.

By early 1796 he was again in New Orleans having secured 250 head of horses which he sold in Natchez and Frankfort. While in Kentucky he visited General Wilkinson who supplied him with Spanish silver. The following year, he launched this third expedition to Texas with a third passport. With him went eight men who would assist him in capturing horses for the Louisiana regiment. During on this somewhat lengthy stay, Nolan and his men managed to collect over 1,200 horses for transport to Louisiana. On this expedition his actions thoroughly aroused the suspicions of authorities in New Spain and caused them to pose serious questions concerning his motives.

Notwithstanding this growing opposition to his forays into Texas, Nolan confidently organized a fourth expedition which in 1800 made its way into the region. On this occasion he was not able to obtain a passport making his expedition a dangerous undertaking. With him came at least twenty-seven well armed men but not well mounted. They made their way across the Sabine and Trinity Rivers well north of Nacogdoches and on to the Brazos River ultimately striking camp in the region of today's McLennan or Hill County where he erected a small fort, built some corrals, and began capturing wild horses. There they found game plentiful and the climate favorable.

Their fort was a roofless enclosure of logs placed one on another to a height of about five feet in which they kept their saddles and clothes and to protect themselves against an Indian attack. Nearby they erected other smaller structures and several corrals. In the neighborhood the adventurers discovered elk and deer in abundance as well as a few buffalo. Wild horses in the thousands also roamed the region. These mustangs tamed and driven to Natchez would claim prices averaging fifty dollars a head.

Spanish officials at Natchez alerted all frontier officers of Nolan's "hostile" intentions. The Spanish commandant at Chihuahua informed the Governor of Texas that his informants in Louisiana assured him that Nolan was a very intelligent individual, but a consummate hypocrite, without any religion although pretending to a Roman Catholic. In another dispatch the commandant at Nacogdoches was informed that Nolan was active, enterprising, and resolute, was better acquainted with the country than the natives themselves, and had with him dangerous characters. The Texas Governor was also informed that Nolan was a heretic, the most dangerous man that ever entered Texas, and should be arrested and closely confined.

Whereupon the Spanish commandant at Chihuahua issued orders for the apprehension of the illegal trespassers, dead or alive. In the spring of 1801, 150 soldiers from the presidio at Nacogdoches sought Nolan's forces. They found Nolan's contingent at some horse pens that tradition has located in an area some thirty miles northeast of the present day City of Waco in McLennan County. Other scholars, however, maintain that Nolan's camp was located in the neighborhood of the Tehuacana Hill in what is now Limestone County.

The Nacogdoches forces were well armed and in addition had brought a swivel cannon mounted on mule back. A pitched battle ensued in which Philip Nolan was slain by a random shot that struck him in the head. In the years after his death, he attained a sort of symbolic status as one of the earliest Texas freedom fighters.

His men were captured, but three of the Anglo Americans and a Negro escaped. The other prisoners, consisting of eight Anglos, one Mexican and one Louisiana creole were taken first to Nacogdoches, then sent to San Antonio in irons, and later imprisoned at San Luis Potosi. After sixteen months in prison there they were moved to Chihuahua, Mexico where they were tried and ordered released. The Commandant of the Internal Provinces objected to the decision, and the matter was referred to Spain. Finally, in 1807, after six years of imprisonment, an order came from Spain that one man of each five should be executed, the choice to be made by lot, and the remainder of the men should serve ten years at hard labor.

This decision meant that two of the ten should be executed but since one of them had died in the meantime, local authorities determined that only one execution would satisfy the order. The nine men cast dice, and Ephriam Blackburn, the oldest of the group, made the losing cast. He was then hanged at Chihuahua in November. The rest of the group were sent to different penal settlements.

One of them, Peter Ellis Bean, was a remarkably resourceful prisoner. In 1810 when revolt broke out in Mexico, Bean volunteered to join the Royal Army and fight for the crown. He was released and soon deserted to the rebel forces. He persuaded the rebel leaders to send him to the United States to gain American sympathy and aid. He arrived in New Orleans in 1814 in time to join General Andrew Jackson's army at the Battle of New Orleans. After Mexico secured independence from Spain in 1821, Bean returned to Mexico, was commissioned a colonel in the Mexican Army, and married a rich Mexican woman.

A deserter from Nolan's forces implied that Nolan planned to make the 1800 expedition a sort of preparation for a more ambitious expedition to be led from Kentucky for the conquest of Texas or perhaps

EARLY EAST TEXAS

New Mexico. Nolan's known close association with General Wilkinson lent credence to this story and helped brand Nolan as a filibusterer. Spanish colonial officials declared that they had papers in their possession that clearly demonstrated that Nolan expected to raise a revolution and make himself ruler of Texas.

    The severe, even brutal, treatment accorded Nolan and his party did little to deter other American adventurers from entering Texas. An abortive Mexican revolution launched in 1810 was suppressed, and as a result the Texas frontier regions were left in a state of relative calm, and the lives of their inhabitants undisturbed. American General Zebulon Pike passing through Texas in 1807 reckoned the total non-Indian population at 7,000, of whom 2,000 were living in the capital city of San Antonio. Nacogdoches he declared was merely a station for troops situated, as he wrongly reported, on a small branch of the Attoyac River.

    The inhabitants of the province, he recalled, were principally Spanish Creoles, some French, some Americans, and a few civilized Indians and half-breeds. Geographically, he contended it was one of "richest, most prolific, and best watered countries in North America. Under these circumstances, American adventurers were lured to cross the Sabine River to hunt for horses and to participate in the lucrative

Indian trade. But others had grander objectives, they looked across the Sabine River and saw political confusion and frustrated opponents of Spanish rule. They gained the notion that with the help of those men that Texas was ripe for conquest.

Magee-Gutiérrez Expedition

One of those American adventurers was Augustus Magee, a lieutenant in the Army of the United States who had been dispatched to the Neutral Ground in 1810 to drive the lawless elements from the strip and restore law and order. Magee, a native of Massachusetts, had been born in 1789 and at age twenty graduated third in his class for the United States Military Academy at West Point. Thereafter, he served under General James Wilkinson in an artillery regiment stationed at Baton Rouge, Louisiana and was later transferred to Fort Jessup near Natchitoches.

While suppressing freebooters and other lawless characters of the Neutral Ground, he became acquainted with Samuel Davenport and Bernardo Gutiérrez de Lara. Three were soon engaged in creating plans for an invasion of Texas. Magee's commanding officer had recommended him for a promotion as one of the best informed young officers in the army, but the promotions was not forthcoming. In 1812, smarting over his failure to gain a promotion and embroiled in the plot to invade Texas, Magee in 1812 resigned his commission and immediately began recruiting the military force that came to be known as the Magee-Gutiérrez Expedition.

Gutiérrez was born in 1774 at Revilla (present-day Guerrero), Tamaulipas, Mexico. By 1810 he was a successful merchant, blacksmith, and property owner in his home town. At that time he and his brother succeeded in raising a revolution in Nuevo Santander, and Bernardo was dispatched to the Rio Grande to recruit others to join the revolutionaries. In 1811, he volunteered to go the United States to solicit aid. A secret council of the principal rebel officers meeting at Saltillo in April 1811 provided him with appropriate documents and dispatches, and later in the month he started for the United States.

An Anglo American contemporary and leading figure in the later Long Expeditions, Henry S. Foote, in an 1841 history, described Gutiérrez as "a professed entertainer of liberal principles," a man possessing a highly commanding person, most insinuating manners, and extraordinary mental accomplishments. He also characterized his co-leader Magee as a man of more than ordinary accomplishments in all respects admirably fitted for the task as commander of a military force bent invasion of foreign territory.

The Mexican rebel went first to Natchitoches and then on to Washington, D. C., with letters of introduction. During his visit to the American capital he talked with the ministers of Britain, Denmark, and Russia. Late in July, Gutiérrez was in Louisiana where he met Captain Jose Alferez Miguel Menchaca, a Mexican Texan who had deserted from the Royalist Army and was fleeing for his life. Gutiérrez recruited the deserter, assembled a party of twelve men, equipped them with arms, munitions, money, and pack animals, and gathered all the gold and silver they could obtain.

They began the trek to Natchitoches in September knowing they needed to avoid contact with Indians and Spaniards. Along the way they persuaded some Indian bands to assist them, but when they entered the Neutral Ground they were confronted by fifty armed Spanish Royalists. Eleven of the party managed to escape but only with their arms. Their documents, dispatches, supplies, and gold and silver were lost.

When the Gutiérrez party reached Natchitoches, they adopted a new set of plans. Menchaca was delegated to assemble a military force and conquer Texas. Gutiérrez would proceed to Washington to seek aid. He reported that the people of the United States were interested in his project and encouraged him to proceed. He also related that he was able to persuade American officials to come to his aid. They offered, he said, to recruit 50,000 men from Tennessee and Kentucky who would march to the Rio Grande and raid the rebels from that location. The offer was withdrawn when Gutiérrez demanded that he be in complete control of the force until a new Mexican government could be formed.

Soon after the American offer was retracted, he learned of treachery by Menchaca, and he immediately boarded ship bound for New Orleans. When in April 1812, Gutiérrez reached the Louisiana port, he immediately set out for Natchitoches where he met Augustus Magee and the two joined forces.

Very soon thereafter, Magee became the leader of the enterprise. Gutiérrez was left in charge in name in order to gain the support of Mexican Texans. When the Mexican arrived in Natchitoches, he met another Anglo American who was interested in joining the Expedition. William Shaler, a special agent dispatched by Secretary of State James Monroe to report on developments, was an American sea captain who furnished valuable assistance and whose help added greatly to the efficiency of the campaign.

While in Natchitoches, Magee and Gutiérrez recruited volunteers for that they were now calling the "Republican Army of the North." Apparently many, if not most of the American volunteers had the idea that Texas was to be an independent nation not merely a pawn in Guiterrez' plan for Mexican independence.

Meanwhile, Samuel Davenport of

EARLY EAST TEXAS

Nacogdoches spent the summer of 1812 gathering provisions and munitions as well as recruiting volunteers. A league of land and forty dollars in American money was promised each volunteer. About 150 residents of the Neutral Ground enlisted ready for any assignment.

In August, 1812, the little army of some 400 men at this time under the command of Gutiérrez began their march westward toward Texas. Spanish forces had taken up a position at a crossing of the Sabine River expecting to turn the American back at that point, but they were outflanked and forced to retreat to their base in Nacogdoches, leaving a patrol of some twenty men at the Attoyac River to spy on the advancing Americans. The filibusterers attacked the Spanish patrol while they were at matins (a Catholic Church service observed at dawn). Only the Spanish sentinel escaped to bear the news to Nacogdoches.

The Mexican commandant ordered breastworks constructed in part from bales of wool intended for the Louisiana market. When the he sounded the alarm expecting all armed citizens of the town to come to the defense of the town, not a citizen responded to his call. On the contrary they seemed indifferent even happy at the prospect of liberty from Spanish rule. The soldiers of the garrison also seemed depressed and indifferent.

Although the Spanish troops were entrenched

EARLY EAST TEXAS

on Orton Hill which overlooked the town on the East, they were thrown into confusion and dismay at the approach of the revolutionary force and fled hurriedly in squads or singly. They did not stop fleeing until they reached Spanish Bluff (Trinidad), a fort on the Trinity River. Only ten of them rode with their commandant to the Trinity River, a distance of eighty miles, which they reached the following day and made camp.

Magee now joined the expedition and assumed command having resigned his commission. Colonel Samuel Davenport and Captain James Gaines soon came up with about 800 men almost every able bodied man east of the Trinity River. Gaines, who was destined to play a major role in the history of East Texas until he joined the California Gold rush in 1849, was born in 1779 in Culpeper, Virginia, a brother of General Edward Pendleton Gaines of the United States Army. He went to Nashville, Tennessee with his brother in 1803 and on to Natchitoches two years later. He then established a mercantile business and ferry on the Sabine. Gaines gained the confidence of the Mexican inhabitants of East Texas and was employed by them as a land surveyor and chosen by them for local offices.

When the Expeditionary force left Nacogdoches, Captain James Gaines was left at the Sabine River crossing to forward new recruits and maintain lines of communication with the forces marching on San Antonio. Before attacking the old provincial capital, the filibusterers planned to subdue Spanish forces at La Bahia (Goliad). From captured scouts they learned that an ambush awaited them at the Guadalupe River crossing. A forced march was ordered, the ambush avoided, and Goliad was captured in mid-November. The Spanish forces returned, surrounded La Bahia, and placed the town under siege for the next four months.

As the siege wore on, clashes between Magee and Gutiérrez led to a permanent rupture between the two leaders, leading to a three-day cessation of hostilities. Unexpectedly, Magee dined with the Spanish commanding officer in the latter's quarters and an agreement was reached. The fort now held by the forces of the Expedition was to be delivered up, and the Americans allowed to return home without their arms but with supplies furnished by the Spaniards.

When the troops of the Expedition learned of the proposal, they unanimously voted against the notion that they surrender their arms and march home. Their refusal precipitated a furious assault by the Spanish forces in which the Royalists captured the town and advanced to the walls of the fort before the Americans rallied and retook the town. The combat lasted into the night, and about midnight on February

6, 1813, Magee took his own life with poison, perhaps to avoid being shot by his own forces.

The siege went on until March 12 when the Spaniards withdrew toward San Antonio, detailing spies along the road to watch the rebel forces who remained at Goliad awaiting reinforcements from Nacogdoches. The following week Rueben Ross arrived with some 100 men, after which the invading force of some 900 men marched on San Antonio. Some eight miles east of San Antonio, the Battle of Rosillo then took place. The Royalists, terrified at the coolness exhibited by the Americans, fled the scene leaving to way to San Antonio open. The next day, April 1, the old town surrendered without further fighting.

Thereafter disagreement among the Expedition's leadership accelerated. Although a civil government was established with its capital at San Antonio in early April, the slaughter of seventeen Royalist leaders provoked considerable disgust among the Americans under Gutiérrez' command, and a large number of them left to return to the United States. Included among those who left were a colonel, a major, and other officers further weakening the leadership of the army. Samuel Davenport, the Expedition's quartermaster left La Bahia perhaps foreseeing the coming end of the revolutionary effort.

Several of the remaining leaders were blamed

EARLY EAST TEXAS

for the massacre of the Royalists, but ultimately Gutiérrez was finally deposed by decision of a tribunal created to place him on trial on charges of treachery and barbarity. Moreover, without strong leadership to impose discipline, the remaining troops abandoned themselves to great excesses. Chaos soon reigned and the Army of the Republic of the North became an unruly mob instead of a well-organized fighting force.

While the rebel troops in San Antonio were running riot, the Spaniards gathered another military force which marched to San Antonio, killed and scattered the Expedition's guards who were grazing horses, and seized those horses. When this news reached them, the invading army became an even more confused mass. On the night of June 4, the army of invaders left San Antonio prepared to attack the Spaniards who were camped near the Alazan River, a branch of the San Pedro River. They surprised the Spanish forces near dawn the following day, and after several hours of hard fighting, the Spanish fled for the Rio Grande leaving behind a thousand dead.

The victorious army returned to San Antonio and elected a new commander causing Gutiérrez to flee toward Natchitoches in fear of his life. Very soon thereafter another Spanish army approached old San Antonio. The rebel army again set forth to attack, but were ambushed by the Royalists, and the Army of the

EARLY EAST TEXAS

North annihilated at La Bahia. The Spanish began a systematic purge calculated to rid Texas of all Anglo-Americans and liberal Mexicans, indeed every friend of the invaders who did not manage to escape across the Sabine River into American Louisiana. Rebels were shot, their property confiscated, and their wives and daughters imprisoned and forced to labor for the Royalist Army. So thoroughly did the Spanish officials exact their revenge that their actions left all of Texas a virtually uninhabited region.

The Magee-Gutiérrez Expedition was a failure, in part, because the difference in ideas concerning its ultimate goals: an independent Texas or a Mexican state of Texas. The War of 1812 between the United States and England prevented greater participation by more American citizens. Virtually all the residents of East Texas were involved to some degree in this attempt to free Texas from Mexican domination, and an unhappy consequence of its failure was the depopulation of East Texas. As the victorious Spanish forces marched eastward, the inhabitants of East Texas fled in terror beyond the Sabine.

The success, however short-lived, of the Republican Army of the North provided many adventurers in the United States with dreams of conquest and glory in the province of Texas. Following the overwhelming defeat of the British forces at New Orleans in 1815, many of them turned

EARLY EAST TEXAS

their attention to the land beyond the Sabine.

For the next six years (1813-1819) the East Texas region remained an uninhabited wasteland. The town of Nacogdoches, for example, that had been so full of life and activity in 1810 had become an almost deserted village. Only a scant few, perhaps less than one hundred, remained to trade with the scattered remnants of the once thriving Indian tribes of East Texas.

Existing documents indicate that in 1818 some settlers, at least a few, had begun to reenter East Texas. For example, Edmund Quirk and his three sons-in-law returned and three of them settled once again in the Ayish Bayou region in present day San Augustine County, while Christobal Chonca transferred his Palo Gacho Bayou plantation in northeastern San Augustine County to Joshua Blair who in turn sold it to Lewis Holloway. But the following year the beginnings of renewed settlement were once again interrupted by invasion and conflict.

That same year the United States and the Kingdom of Spain entered into the Florida Purchase Treaty whereby the Spanish territory known as Florida was ceded to the United States and the Sabine River designated as the official boundary between the two nations. Despite the ease with which the treaty was ratified by the United States Senate, there was strong opposition in the Old Southwest Territory. Large numbers of persons, many of them influential citizens, held vehemently to the belief that Congress had no constitutional power to sell, exchange, or relinquish an "American possession" as they regarded the province of Texas.

The Long Expeditions

A number of protest meetings were scheduled that were attended by many prominent men, especially along the Mississippi River. As an outgrowth, in the spring of 1919, the people of Natchez, Mississippi organized and equipped an expedition to invade and conquer Texas and establish there an independent republic. At the meeting Dr. James Long, a well-regarded Natchez physician, was chosen to lead the proposed expedition.

Long was a native Virginian, born in Culpeper County about 1793. His parents migrated first to Kentucky and then to Maury County, Tennessee. At age fifteen he unsuccessfully engaged in the mercantile business, then clerked in his father's store for two years, and finally saved some $200 which allowed him to study medicine under a Tennessee physician. He thereby acquired enough medical knowledge to join the U. S. Army as a surgeon. He served as a surgeon in General William Carrol's

EARLY EAST TEXAS

brigade in General Andrew Jackson's Army at the Battle of New Orleans. At the close of the War of 1812 he moved to Natchez and practiced medicine at Port Gibson for a time.

Shortly after settling in Natchez he met and married Jane Herbert Wilkinson, niece of General James Wilkinson. At his new wife's urging he purchased a plantation near Vicksburg, abandoned the practice of medicine, and soon entered into partnership with W. W. Walker in the mercantile business. One of his advisors who had taken part in the ill-fated expeditions into Texas described Long as a man who was by nature a soldier always looking for an opportunity to indulge in military exploits.

Dr. Long soon recruited seventy-five men, and in mid June set out from Natchez to invade Spanish Texas. Recruits were attracted to the venture by the usual prospect of an exciting adventure and by the promise of a league of land to every one who enrolled. As the little band marched west their number grew until it reached 300 by the time it reached the Sabine River and Texas. Long and his fighting men passed through Natchitoches on their way to the border and the town of Nacogdoches. When he arrived at the Spanish outpost in late June his army had swelled to some 600 Americans and Mexicans and a large number of Indians.

The citizens of Nacogdoches and vicinity

assembled that same day and proceeded to create a provisional government composed of twenty-one members who elected General Long President of the Supreme Council and commander-in-chief of the armed forces. Long accepted the position, appealed for the cooperation of all interested in freeing Texas, and pledged to carry out his duties with all his abilities. Other members of the Supreme Council included Bernardo Gutiérrez and Samuel Davenport, two of the leaders of the ill-fated Magee-Gutiérrez Expedition.

Underlying all the rhetoric and fervent pronouncements lay the chief motive that animated the leaders and many, if not most, of the rank and file of the Long Expedition, the desire for land. They saw themselves a vanguard that would get possession of Texas and open it to Anglo-American settlement. This motivation was underscored by the October decree of the Supreme Council offering each private who entered the service before the following October ten sections of land as soon as the government was settled.

The Council also authorized the survey and sale of lands on the Attoyac and Red Rivers. The minimum price fixed for those along the Attoyac was one dollar per acre, payable one-fourth down and the balance in three annual installments. Lands along the Red River were to sell for various sums according to their quality ranging from twenty-five cents to fifty cents per acre.

The same month the Council declared Galveston a port of entry and delivery and authorized the erection of a fort on Bolivar Point. The notorious pirate Jean Laffite was commissioned as governor of Galveston to cement his willingness to assist in the operations of the Expedition. Long did not know that Laffite was plotting to betray him, and left his headquarters in Nacogdoches late in October with thirteen men bent on going to Galveston.

On his way to the Gulf of Mexico Long learned that a Spanish punitive force was headed toward East Texas, and he immediately made haste to return to Nacogdoches. Upon arrival at the Spanish outpost, he found the town entirely deserted. Although Spanish authority in Texas was virtually nonexistent in 1819 and the invaders had every reason to believe they would succeed, Long made a fatal tactical error. He proceeded to divide his small force into detachments which were scattered widely over East Texas. A Spanish military force of some 550 men left San Antonio in late September with orders to overcome the invading force.

Spies were dispatched to investigate conditions in Nacogdoches. They soon returned with a report that Long's main force was concentrated on the Sabine River more than thirty miles east of the settlement and that the two locations were virtually undefended. The Spaniards advanced cautiously, and their slow advance gave the invaders enough time to escape had their intelligence service been operating as it should.

Royalist forces captured ten of Long's men as they neared Nacogdoches, and the remainder of their march was a succession of raids against small Anglo-American parties. Nacogdoches was not much of a prize when at last it fell to the Spaniards. General Long arrived too late to prevent the capture of the town, and late in the month left for the Sabine River and safety before he could be captured.

Bringing peace to the region continued through November until most of ranchos were destroyed. Anglo-Americans were driven away from the Atascosito settlement on the Trinity River in present day Liberty County, and elsewhere in East Texas and at least twenty of their homes destroyed by fire. Some of Long's recruits found refuge at Galveston, but most of them crossed the Sabine River to safety in the United States.

After Long's unsuccessful invasion collapsed, the eastern third of Texas was again destitute. There were not more than 4,000 Europeans and Americans in all of the province. Extant documents indicate that east of San Antonio all signs of civilization that remained after the disaster of the Magee-Gutiérrez

EARLY EAST TEXAS

Expedition were themselves swept away.

Dr. Long took his wife to Natchitoches and then returned to Texas where he met with some of his men at Bolivar Point. There he learned of their desperate need for supplies and proceeded immediately to New Orleans and back to Natchitoches. Long thereafter returned to Bolivar Point where he issued a proclamation requesting all members of his army to report to him in the Point by mid April. With some difficulty Long secured funds for assembling a second effort at subduing Texas.

About fifty recruits were prevented from joining him by United States Marshals in Louisiana, but John Austin, a distant relative of Empressario Stephen F. Austin, and Benjamin Rush Milam, an adventuresome veteran of the War of 1812, joined him and figured prominently in Long's effort and in subsequent Texas history.

Long was impatient to make an assault on La Bahia, but friends and supporters persuaded him to wait until enough Anglo-Americans could come to Texas to guarantee success. Meanwhile his small army built a fort on Bolivar Point and declared that Galveston was an official port of entry for then Republic of Texas. At last, deeming the time ripe for attack, in September Long and his force of fifty-two men entered La Bahia without resistance. The Spanish governor immediately dispatched a military force to

EARLY EAST TEXAS

demand the surrender of Long and his men. In early October after only harmless exchange of fire, Long surrendered.

The prisoners were taken to San Antonio and imprisoned. In time, Long was transferred to a prison in Mexico City. While he was in prison, in 1821 Mexico gained its independence from Spain. Because Long had claimed, among other goals, to be fighting to secure that end, the American ambassador was able to secure his release from prison. Thereafter, while walking down the street in the Mexican capital, he was shot by a Mexican soldier under suspicious circumstances.

The defeat of Long's expedition again brought disaster to the East Texas settlements and their residents. The settlements were wiped out and their inhabitants driven off by military force. When shortly thereafter Mexico won its independence, the scattered settlers were able to again trickle back across the Sabine to their abandoned homes. They discovered that the land had been wasted by some eight years of turmoil and fighting. They optimistically hailed Mexican independence as a release from Spanish official delays and burdensome restrictions on trade and commerce.

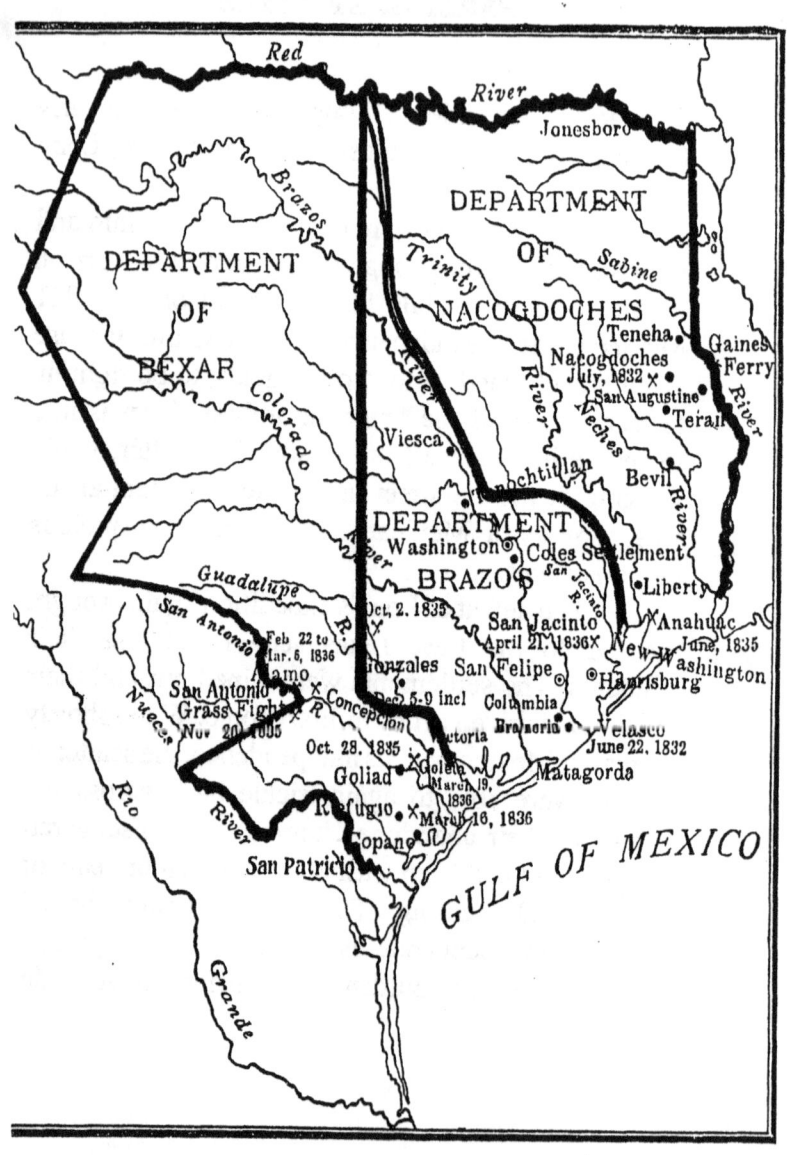

TEXAS IN 1835.

CHAPTER THREE

THE FREDONIAN REBELLION

Wednesday. November 22, 1826. On this fall day a small band of armed men, thirty-five to forty in number, rode westward through the pine forest along the old Royal Road (El Camino Real), across the Ayish Bayou on their way to the old Spanish outpost of Nacogdoches now a Mexican town and garrison. Nestled between two every running creeks (Banita and La Nana), it had been inhabited by Europeans for varying lengths of time for over a century.

Despite its rather long existence as a European settlement, the number of inhabitants in Nacogdoches had varied from virtually 900 according to a Mexican census taken in 1806 to a low of just 200 demonstrated by a similar 1823 count. Thus, when Haden Edwards came in 1825 to assume authority over his grant, comparatively few people were located within its limits. Most of the non-Indian people residing in East Texas were located in a band of land sixty miles in width between the eastern extremity of his grant and the Sabine River.

The riders were bent on ousting the Mexican

EARLY EAST TEXAS

officials, particularly the Alcalde, Samuel Norris[3], and the Sindico, Jose Antonio Sepulveda whom they believed had not been legally elected to office. They succeeded in capturing those two but failed to apprehend James Gaines, who headed a group calling themselves the Regulators whose objective was to enforce the decisions of his brother-in law Alcalde Norris.

This bunch of disgruntled Anglo-Americans, perhaps unwittingly, had touched off a series of events that in the next decade would culminate in freeing the eastern region of the province of Texas from Mexican control and fueling the flames of the Texas Revolution. They were led by two of the more colorful characters who had entered the Nacogdoches-San Augustine district after 1821 when Texas was opened to American colonization.

Their commander, Colonel Martin Parmer, was a recent arrival who had come from Missouri by

---

[3] Norris, native of St. Mary's County, Maryland, was born there in 1783. With his parents he immigrated to Natchez, Mississippi in 1802 and the next year to a rancho near the Attoyac River in present-day Nacogdoches County. After a brief absence, he returned to Nacogdoches in 1820 where in 1825 he was elected the alcalde of the community.

EARLY EAST TEXAS

way of the Arkansas Post. He had lost his wife of many years soon after coming to the Mexican state of Coahuila y Texas. Now at loose ends the colonel in keeping with his reputation as the "Ring Tailed Panther" of Missouri was eager and ready for a fight. A contemporary remembered that Parmer had arrived in Texas in a reckless state of mind, ready for anything that might turn up. Other contemporaries described him as a stern, rough man, imperious and dominating in disposition. He had gained some notoriety in Missouri as an Indian fighter and spinner of dynamic tales. Since coming in contact with the people in East Texas, he had acquired a noticeable distaste for Mexicans in general.

His second in command, Major John S. Roberts, was a veteran of the War of 1812 who in 1826 had come to East Texas from Louisiana. Major Roberts had already proven that he was a man of action who was easily attracted to any armed action in his neighborhood.

Antecedents: The Reentry

This November march on Nacogdoches was the outgrowth of developments in the history of Mexican Texas that had their immediate cause in a decision in 1824 by officials in Mexico City to allow, even encourage, Anglo-American immigration. They

EARLY EAST TEXAS

were driven to this potentially dangerous expedient by their growing conviction that unless the frontier regions of Texas were soon populated the new Republic of Mexico would see them fall into other hands. The aggressive land-hungry Anglo Americans were poised on the eastern border just across the Sabine River and European nations (Germany, France, and England) beginning to show interest.

From the earliest days of Spanish acquisition of the territory, official policy had demonstrated a determination to prohibit immigration of foreign subjects. Except for brief periods of time such as the years from 1762 to 1800 when France ceded the Louisiana Territory to Spain foreign subjects could not legally enter Texas to become settlers. From time to time, however, special permission was granted to individuals such as the merchants and Indian traders William Barr and Samuel Davenport in Nacogdoches. In any event by the time of the Mexican Revolution in 1821 a number of European and American immigrants had obtained legal entry.

Two new elements emerged in the history of East Texas in the years surrounding Mexican Independence. Spanish missionaries, soldiers, and colonists as well as English and Irish adventurers and traders were gradually overshadowed by hundreds of land hungry Anglo Americans. In addition, the friendly Caddo Indians of early colonial times disappear and are replaced by new tribes arriving from the Southeastern region of the United States.

Foremost among these new Indian immigrants were the Cherokees. For more than a century they had been in contact with Europeans originally in the Carolinas and Georgia but later also in Tennessee. Long before the advent of the Europeans these native Americans had been a domestic sedentary tribe living in towns and villages, cultivating the soil, and achieving a significant measure of civilization. As the Anglos pushed inland they encountered these settled tribes who were reluctant to give up their land. As a consequence a series of Indian wars broke out as the Cherokees defended their territory against encroachment.

Finally, worn out by continuous warfare, their traditional hunting grounds occupied by the invading European immigrants, and their villages greatly reduced in population, families and small parties of dissatisfied Cherokees immigrated to the lands of their friend and ally Spain, settling on the White River in the Louisiana Territory. After the United States purchased Louisiana in 1803, they sought the consent of President Thomas Jefferson for permission to continue to settle in the territory.

By the end of 1819 some 6,000 Cherokees had moved west of the Mississippi River. As they drifted westward, this large contingent of Cherokees created

EARLY EAST TEXAS

conflict with the Indian tribes whose hunting grounds they appropriated, and they also troubled the Europeans there who were opposed to seeing their fertile agricultural lands closed to other settlers by the presence of the Indians. The American government intervened and sought to maintain peace and order. But by 1809 the Indians had begun packing up their trappings and leaving for Spanish Texas.

In 1818 or 1819, a small band of some sixty of their number separated from the main body and crossed the Sabine River into East Texas. They settled between the Trinity and Sabine Rivers north of Nacogdoches and the Old San Antonio Road. This advance party was soon joined by remnants of Shawnees, Delawares, Kickapoos, and other tribes.

Along with others of their tribe these Indians were determined to escape the unfriendly domination of Anglo-Americans. They were not savages as they were painted by the Americans they encountered in the Old Southwest. They practiced a primitive agriculture in addition to hunting game and other wildlife, tending therefore, to lead a sedentary life and to remain in a fairly well established territory. They made their own cloth from which they fashioned their clothing, raised cattle and horses, used firearms. Many of them understood the English and Spanish languages as well as their own.

They had learned from their experiences with

EARLY EAST TEXAS

European settlers that a legal title from the government was necessary to obtain permanent possession of the land. Very soon after their arrival in Texas they began making application to the Spanish government for a royal grant giving them title to the lands they had occupied. The Cherokees petitioned royal authorities to grant them land as a tribe and permit them to set up their own government. Permission was not forthcoming, but they were assured that if they waited patiently their request would be granted.

In their dealings with Spanish officials in San Antonio and Mexico City, the Indians' spokesmen were Richard Fields and John Dunn Hunter. In their earliest dealings with the Spanish Fields acted alone, but in later negotiations with the Mexicans Hunter joined him. Fields was a half-breed who had gained at least an elementary education and who possessed a considerable fund of common sense. Fields had been born about 1762 in Spartanburg, South Carolina and was thus an older man when as one of their chiefs he led people into Eastern Texas.

Hunter was a well-traveled native of Scotland who was born about 1796. In one of his volumes of Mexican history, H. H. Bancroft wrote that Hunter did not remember his parents, whom he believed were slain by Indians when he was captured as a young boy. In like fashion, he did not know where or when the

EARLY EAST TEXAS

tragedy had occurred. His skill as a hunter during his boyhood was greatly admired by his Indian captors who gave him the name Hunter. He added the names John Dunn after a Missourian of the same name who befriended him as a young boy.

Hunter left off living with the Indians in 1816 when he joined a group of fur traders and attended school for a time near Pearl River, Mississippi. In 1821 he went to New York and later traveled to London where he was lionized. After his return to the United States he devoted his life to promoting civilization and knowledge among his Indian friends. In 1825, he wandered into the Cherokee settlement in East Texas.

When the Cherokees entered Texas their war chieftain was Bowles (The Bowl), a half breed, who had been born in North Carolina about 1756. He became a friend of San Houston and other Texas leaders and died tragically in the Cherokee War in the 1830s.

The influx of white Anglo Americans that began in earnest about 1820 was a segment of the slow but irresistible progress of a nation of persons who believed that the continent was theirs to occupy. Their most outstanding characteristic was that they came to stay, to take possession of the land, and make it their homesteads. They came looking for a place to "put down roots," and they were willing, even eager,

EARLY EAST TEXAS

to do whatever was necessary to make it happen.

They came under no inducement but the persistent urge of the American pioneer to go forward which meant go westward. The wave of settlement they generated had reached the Sabine River and began crossing over it as they had countless streams in the past. They were willing to disregard the differences in government and legal institutions they encountered in the Spanish province and later the Mexican state. They were the spearhead of a swell permanent settlers that was destined to absorb all other peoples in its path and make Texas what it later became.

A wide variety of types of individuals were represented among these new arrivals. Probably most were sturdy yeoman farmers who knew how to make the soil yield them a living; others were businessmen seeking for chances to make a living from trade; and yet others were lawyers some of whom were gifted with eloquence and possessed great learning. Some were poor attracted by the offer of cheap land where they could start a new life; others were comparatively rich and brought their wealth with them.

Some were well educated while others were persons of less learning but anxious to provide learning for their children. Many were persons of deep religious commitment but who could not openly practice their Protestant faiths until Mexican garrisons were expelled in the early years of the decade of the 1830s.

In the face of the need to repopulate Texas following the successful conclusion of the Mexican Revolution in 1821 and this new invasion of restless Anglo Americans, the response of the Mexican government was initially pragmatic and tolerant. Quite probably their belief was that since they could not stem the tide of Anglo American immigration, then they should seek to exert some control over it. The outgrowth of this line of reasoning was a series of colonization laws promulgated in the decade of the 1820s.

In August 1824 the Mexican national Congress enacted a general colonization law for the nation. The federal statute turned over the administration of the public lands to the Mexican states and authorized them to prescribe regulations to govern them. Earlier that same year, the old Spanish provinces of Coahuila and Texas were united as one state until the population of Texas warranted a separate state government. The next year the government at Saltillo promulgated a colonization law for the state.

The Colonization Law of 1825 initiated a system whereby individual immigrants who gave satisfactory evidence of their Christian beliefs, morality, and good habits could receive, after paying several small fees, a league of land (more than 4,425 acres). To perfect their claim to the land, they were required to cultivate or occupy the land within six years following application. Families and combinations of individuals could also obtain land through the empresario system. Empresarios who recruited immigrants could receive for their services five leagues of grazing land and five labors (a labor was 177 acres) of farming land (a total of more than 22,000 acres of grazing land and 885 acres of farming land) for each 100 families to a maximum of 800 families. Potentially then empresarios could obtain more than 175,000 acres for each fulfilled empresario contract.

An Empresario Comes

Among those avidly seeking empresario contracts was Haden Edwards, a Virginia-born plantation owner and land speculator. From a plantation in Hinds County, Mississippi, Edwards had later acquired a Louisiana plantation. In 1825, his petition was approved and he received an empresario grant for land in East Texas based on the old Spanish settlement of Nacogdoches. Three important conditions were attached to the Edwards grant: all existing Spanish and Mexican land titles granted to individuals were to be honored, a militia for the

EARLY EAST TEXAS

protection of the region should be organized, and a land commission should be formed to convey title to lands after 100 families had been settled.

The Edwards grant presented its empresario with a number of serious problems. On the east Edwards had to contend with the inhabitants of the neutral Strip on the Louisiana side of the Sabine River, on the southwest his boundary joined the not well established boundary of Stephen F. Austin's colony, and on his north and west were situated several Indian tribes, notably the Cherokees only recently driven from their ancestral homes in the southeastern part of the United States. In addition, the town of Nacogdoches contained a number of potential troublemakers including veterans of earlier filibustering expeditions and long-time Mexican residents not entirely pleased about having themselves and their land included within the boundaries of the Edwards grant.

The East Texas empresario had been born in Stafford County, Virginia August 12, 1771, one of eleven children of John and Susannah Wroe Edwards. Along with other members of his family, Haden left Virginia in the later years of the century. They took up residence near Paris, Bourbon County, Kentucky where Grandfather Haden had already settled. While there are few reliable facts concerning the early life of the empresario, there is general agreement that he studied law and was destined for a legal career. During the same years he also absorbed from his father's actions the attraction of land speculation and the operation of a plantation.

He began engaging in western land speculation as early as 1789 becoming involved in the land deals of the flamboyant Baron Felipe Enrique Neri de Bastrop in the Louisiana Territory. In any event, by about 1815 he had become a man with considerable assets who continued to dabble in land speculation. While doing so, he acquired a large plantation on the Pearl River in Hinds County, Mississippi where he soon moved his family and his slaves.

His family consisted of his wife, Susannah Beall, daughter of Charles and Tabitha (Beall) Beall, whom he had married in Kentucky about 1798, along with seven sons and five daughters. At least four of his daughters married men who were destined to be important actors in the history of East Texas. Susan Wroe Edwards married Frost Thorn who became one of the region's first millionaires; Elizabeth Turner Edwards married Herman B. Mayo, a prominent figure in the Fredonian Rebellion; Tabitha Beall Edwards married Chichester Chaplin, a lawyer and prominent political figure in both East Texas and Western Louisiana; while Jane Edwards married first Juan Bernardo Davenport, son of Samuel and prominent merchant. One of his sons, Haden Harrison

EARLY EAST TEXAS

Edwards, became a well-known political, legal, and military figure in the last years of the Republic of Texas and the early years of statehood.

In 1825, political authority in all of Texas was vested in the government of the Department of Bexar which consisted of a Political Chief appointed by the governor of the Mexican State of Coahuila y Texas. He was to reside at the old colonial capital of San Antonio and was charged with the duty of maintaining public tranquility throughout the territory. He also had authority to inflict criminal punishments, to command the local militia, to issue and examine passports, to preside over popular meetings and festivities, to resolve all problems brought to him by his associates, to serve as the sole channel between his subordinates and the state government, and to report his actions and his observations to the state governor. His department was divided into a series of municipalities, of which the Municipality of Nacogdoches was one with jurisdiction over a large portion of the area between the Trinity and Sabine Rivers.

Each municipality was governed by an elected Alcalde, an executive officer who combined many of the functions of a mayor, sheriff, and justice of the peace. He was assisted by an Ayuntamiento (town council) elected by the qualified residents of the municipality. In addition, Stephen F. Austin with his

EARLY EAST TEXAS

headquarters located at San Felipe was designated the chief judge to whom appeals could be made from any alcalde's jurisdiction. Thus, Edwards was legally subject to the authority of the Nacogdoches alcalde and to Austin, the ultimate authority in legal matters.

In 1825, when Haden Edwards first arrived in East Texas, there were few persons within the boundaries of his grant which ranged from twenty leagues north of the Gulf of Mexico on the south, to twenty leagues west of then Sabine River on the east, to fifteen leagues north of Nacogdoches on the north, and to the Navasota River on the west. Most of inhabitants in this area were settled in a band sixty miles in width between the eastern limit of his grant and the Sabine River.

This border strip contained some 1,600 persons by 1825 encompassing at least 168 families. They comprised a mixture of races, social classes, good and bad characters, criminals from the old Neutral Strip just across the Sabine, Spanish and French Creoles, rough Anglo-American frontiersmen, substantial planters from the Old South of the United States, and fragments of a number of Indian tribes. Into this preexisting confused and potential explosive situation, Edwards was required to operate his empresario enterprise. He was required to respect the rights of the earlier settlers but they were not easily and clearly identifiable.

EARLY EAST TEXAS

The Edwards grant was so extensive in area that those who had been residents in the area for many years were not able to understand what claims the empresario had that were superior to theirs. They also feared that Edwards would be inclined to disturb them in the enjoyment of control over the region that they had exercised without interference from others. The Spanish speaking population resented that an Anglo American was coming into their midst, armed with considerable authority, bent on bring in a flood of immigrants from the United States of whom they already had a greater number than they could control.

While he resided temporarily in Mexico City and Saltillo seeking his grant, Edwards demonstrated prudence, tact, patience, and consideration for those with whom he came in contact. Toward high-ranking aristocratic Mexican politicians he displayed the code of behavior and the social graces of a well-bred Kentucky gentleman. But when the was given his grant and took up residence in Nacogdoches, he apparently abandoned these characteristics.

In dealing with the Spanish speaking element in his grant, especially in the town of Nacogdoches, he displayed neither consideration nor patience. He attempted to use his power to rid his grant of the less prosperous older settlers of whatever station or type and replace them with wealthier planters and others of his liking. In keeping with many of his Anglo-

EARLY EAST TEXAS

American contemporaries from the Old South, he was convinced of the superiority of his class of Southern gentleman and determined to attract to his colony as many of them as possible.

The most pressing and troublesome problem facing Edwards when he arrived in Nacogdoches was the matter of land titles. Within his grant there were already persons living on land he had been granted. Many of them were residing there illegally, and still others could not produce valid titles or other proof of ownership. A good number of them had old Spanish grants, many of which had not been recorded since 1821 when Mexico gained her independence, and others whose titles had been granted by tacit agreement, and which they had held for generations. A few possessed titles granted by Stephen F. Austin's land commissioner in the mistaken belief that the land lay within Austin's grant. Finally, there was an unknown number of squatters without a shred of legality attaching to their possession of the land on which they lived

Believing that his empresario grant authorized him to determine the validity of land claims, Edwards acted mistakenly on this belief. At the principal street corners in Nacogdoches he posted a notice requiring all who claimed previous land grants from Spanish or Mexican governments to come forward immediately and validate their claims with hard legal evidence or their lands would be seized and sold to the highest bidder. In time, not satisfied with the response to then initial notice, a second was posted.

Exactly how many valid claims existed cannot with accuracy be determined, but the threat of confiscation announced by the empresario jeopardized all claims in the minds of the old settlers and placed most of them in opposition to Edward's authority. Despite their alarm and opposition, the empresario stubbornly proceeded to execute his stated intention. He compounded his problem by contending that he had a right to collect a land title fee from those who had been in the colony long before his contract was awarded. The older settlers understandably resented his attempts to collect from them which resulted in escalation of their ill will. Edwards possessed no legal authority to collect land fees since the state government had not yet established a fixed fee for the sale or ownership of land.

Before Edwards arrived to take possession of his grant, Luis Procela, alcalde by proxy in Nacogdoches, and Jose Antonio Sepulveda, the local sindico, moved quickly to validate a number of old Spanish and Mexican land titles which had lain dormant for many years. When the new empresario learned of their actions he accused them of manufacturing fake deeds and forging titles for many of the older settlers. Here again, he mistakenly assumed that he had legal authority to validate all such claims, when, in fact, that task was legally vested in a land commissioner to be appointed by the Mexican authorities.

Shortly after provoking antagonism over validation of land titles, Edwards made a tactical error by calling for an election on December 15, 1825 to name local militia officers. Jose Antonio Sepulveda, an Edwards opponent, was chosen Captain of Militia. Apparently ignoring the outcome of the election, Edwards further assumed that his empresario contract granted him the authority to become the leader of any military forces within the limits of his grant. Although technically he may have had such power, his announced position embittered a considerable number of the area's inhabitants who resented his high handed disregard of their wishes.

Furthermore, he again acted on a mistaken assumption when he called for a second election for January 1, 1826 to select an alcalde for Nacogdoches. A spirited campaign ensued with two candidates contending for the office: Chichester Chaplin,[4] a

---

[4] Chaplin had been born November 17, 1800 in Ireland. After the death of his first wife, Tabitha Beall Edwards, he married Emily Parmer, daughter of Martin Parmer. He later had a distinguished career

young Anglo American lawyer and son-in-law of Edwards, and Samuel Norris, an Anglo American who had married a Spanish colonial who sided with the original settlers.

Chaplin was declared the winner of the 1826 alcalde election, only to have Norris contest the election on the grounds that most of Chaplin's vote came from unqualified persons. The Political Chief in San Antonio reviewed the appeal and declared Norris the winner. After Norris took office, his lack of training and education made him an unpopular choice especially with the Anglo American newcomers.

By April 1826, the empresario was confronted by the fact that both of the major offices in his grant were held by men who were members of the opposition party. Thereafter, more or less constant friction arose between the two political factions, one headed by Edwards and the other by Norris.

During this period of political unrest, Haden's brother, Benjamin Edwards, arrived on the scene. Benjamin Wroe Edwards, a Kentucky native, was a veteran of the War of 1812 in the Canadian campaign of General William Henry Harrison. At war's end he returned to Kentucky where he remained until about 1825 when he immigrated to Jackson, Hinds County,

---

as an attorney and judge in Louisiana and Southeastern Texas.

Mississippi. There he studied law and acquired a reputation for his flights of eloquence and his military exploits.

Contemporaries of Benjamin Edwards maintained that he possessed many admirable qualities, among them modesty and unobtrusive manners. They also commented on his acquaintance with books and human nature. Haden soon prevailed upon his brother to remain in Texas while he went to Louisiana and Mississippi to recruit colonists and financial backing for his colonizing enterprise.

Before leaving for the United States, Haden placed Benjamin in charge of his affairs in Texas, and as time passed Haden's deputy demonstrated that he was less able to deal with the problems that had arisen in the colony. Benjamin simply did not sympathize with the Spanish speaking settlers, could not understand their language, and failed to treat them with either patience or tact. Moreover, he likely viewed the influx of Anglo Americans into Texas but the prelude to ultimate independence and annexation to the territory of the United States. Because of that conviction believed he should provide all the encouragement toward that end he could muster.

Between April and October 1826 disputes over land multiplied and became more critical. Disagreements over ownership were regularly resolved in favor of the older settlers by Alcalde

EARLY EAST TEXAS

Samuel Norris. In addition, a band of "Regulators" under the leadership of James Gaines began a campaign of harassment directed toward those who opposed Norris. An Anglo American historian who was in Texas during this time described this and other such bands as interested primarily in "spoilation and robbery." By October while Haden was still absent Alcalde Norris informed Benjamin that his authority to grant land and charge fees had been revoked.

Advised by Stephen F. Austin to communicate with the Political Chief in San Antonio, Benjamin wrote a series of letters which because of their tone served only to antagonize high-ranking Mexican officials in both San Antonio and Saltillo. Governor Victor Blanco was so outraged by letters he received that he determined to cancel the Edwards empresario contract. He informed Benjamin of his decision in October and ordered the Edwards brothers to leave Texas immediately leaving any unfinished business unfinished.

At this point Haden returned with a report that he had recruited 800 families from Louisiana, Mississippi, Alabama, Tennessee, and Kentucky. But on arrival in Nacogdoches, he was informed that the Governor had annulled his contract. Understandably Haden Edwards believed he had been unfairly treated and that he had been grossly insulted by Governor Blanco.

EARLY EAST TEXAS

In this frame of mind, he determined to retain his lands by detaching East Texas from Mexican control. His determination triggered an armed revolt that came to known as the Fredonian Rebellion.

A Rebellion Launched

The opening act of that revolt was played out in Nacogdoches after the band of men led by Colonel Parmer and Major Roberts rode into the old town, arrested Alcalde Norris and Sindico Sepulveda, placed the empresario and his brother on their parole of honor, and convened a court martial to deal with Norris and Sepulveda. The court consisting of Presiding Judge Colonel Martin Parmer, Major John S. Roberts, Captain Burrell J. Thompson, John W. Mayo, and William Jones found both men guilty of oppression, corruption, and other high crimes, removed them from office, and declared them ineligible to hold office the remainder of their lives. Edward's son-in-law, Herman B. Mayo, served as clerk and Judge Advocate. To fill the alcalde's office until another election could be held the court appointed Joseph Durst.

When news of the capture of Nacogdoches by rebel forces reached San Antonio, a detachment of Mexican troops composed of 110 infantrymen left the provincial capital December 11 with intent to restore order in Nacogdoches and the surrounding area. Reinforced by 250 militiamen from Austin's colony, the force marched from San Felipe on January 22 and arrived in Nacogdoches on February 8 along with 150 other volunteers from the Anglo American settlements in the Ayish Bayou district.

Before those Mexican forces could reach Nacogdoches, on December 16, 1826, Benjamin Edwards rode into the town with some thirty followers and precipitated the Fredonian Rebellion. Under a flag inscribed "Independence, Liberty, and Justice," they took possession of the Old Stone House and proclaimed the Republic of Fredonia. A formal Declaration of Independence was drafted and signed Christmas Day by the Edwards brothers and a council of allies.

In the meantime, Haden Edwards sought the aid of two East Texas Cherokee Indian chiefs: Richard Fields and John Dunn Hunter. He had become acquainted with the men when the Indians were residing in Mexico City where they were also attempting to obtain a grant for their people. Near the first of the New Year these Indian leaders also subscribed to the Declaration of Independence.

In return for their participation in the rebellion, the Cherokees were promised all the country west of the Bexar-Nacogdoches road from Red River to the Rio Grande. The Indians were prompted to join the Edwards attempt since they had been unable to obtain a grant or even assurances from the Mexican government that they should be given legal title to the East Texas lands they occupied.

    The Edwards brothers also appealed to citizens of the United States and to the resident of the Ayish Bayou District to join their forces. When those Anglo Americans failed to respond to their appeal, Haden Edwards made a disastrous mistake. He dispatched two companies of his forces east of the Attoyac River into present day San Augustine County and threatened to confiscate the property of those settlers. Whereupon, in January 1826 a force consisting of Anglo Americans in that area along with some Indian allies captured the Fredonians that had been sent to subdue them.

    Capture of his forces on the Attoyac River and the rapid approach of the Mexican militia and their allies caused their Edwards brothers and most of their cohorts to flee eastward across the Sabine River into the United States and safety. Their Cherokee Indian followers were not so fortunate. Many of them, including Hunter and Fields paid with their lives for the part they played in the Fredonian Rebellion. They were tried by a Cherokee tribunal, found guilty, and executed.

    By December 18, 1826, a force estimated at between fifty and 200 men had assembled in Nacogdoches to support the uprising. Many of them were not avid revolutionaries rather they were attempting to protect their homes from possible confiscation by Mexican authorities. Many of them, including two of their ranking officers, Colonel Parmer and Major Roberts, abandoned the effort as soon as they became convinced that the rebellion would be crushed.

Those of Edwards' people who remained behind were treated reasonably well by the Mexican authorities. An intelligent and patriotic Mexican citizen, Encarnacion Chireno, was made alcalde at Nacogdoches in place of Norris who fled the country, and local government was reestablished on a basis of peace and justice.

EARLY EAST TEXAS

CHAPTER FOUR

TRANQUIL YEARS

Although turmoil and unrest prevailed in the Nacogdoches District west of the Attoyac throughout the early 1820s, relative calm and tranquility reigned in that narrow strip of land between the Sabine River and the Nacogdoches area. The Mexican Colonization Law of 1825 specified that no land would be granted within twenty leagues (52.6 miles) of the border or ten leagues (26.3 miles) of the Gulf coast. The distance from Nacogdoches to the Sabine River was about 58 miles which meant that individuals could not secure legal title to land within that limit.

While colonists that settled in Austin's colony and those who immigrated to other colonies rapidly received deeds to their lands and were allowed to take possession of them, except for the brief and troubled episode of Haden Edwards in Nacogdoches. there was no empresario in East Texas. There almost every settler came on his own initiative and met his own expenses. In this territory no legal provision was made for putting the colonization law into execution, there were no agents empowered to convey land titles, and no one with authority to put immigrants in legal possession of their lands.

EARLY EAST TEXAS

Thus, in this region each immigrant appropriated such land as he wanted, enclosed his fields, built his house, and made such other improvements as seemed appropriate to him. These improvements were the only property the colonist legal held, aside from their personal possessions, and they were bought, sold, or abandoned when the owner wished. As there were no legal titles to convey, no records were kept, and the only title that any man could have to his land was the squatter's title that he lived upon it.

The Red Lands

In 1691, a Spanish exploration led by Domingo Teran de los Rios marked a path through the Red Lands of East Texas that would ultimately become the Old San Antonio Road. His exploration and others later led to the founding in 1717 to the Mission Nuestra Señora de los Ais on the Ayish Bayou near present day San Augustine. Three years later drought, hunger, lack of supplies, and the threat of French encroachment brought about its abandonment. But in 1722 it was rebuilt on Mission Hill near the Bayou where it remained until finally abandoned in 1773 when the Spanish abandoned all of East Texas.

In 1779, along with the return of Gill Y'Barbo

EARLY EAST TEXAS

and other former residents of Nacogdoches and Los Adaes new and former residents moved into the area they called the Ayish Bayou. Most of these early settlers, especially those who determined to make their homes in the forbidden twenty league strip east of Nacogdoches, came and went without leaving a record of their presence. The refusal of Spanish and Mexican governments to grant land titles did little to discourage immigrants, both Spanish and Anglo Americans from making their homes in the area. Most of the American immigrants, including Indians, came from Mississippi, Alabama, Georgia, Tennessee, and Kentucky.

Those who came to the area now designated as San Augustine, Sabine, and Shelby Counties, but then generally known as the Ayish Bayou District, came as a result of a number of factors. Perhaps the most compelling of these was the existence of a well-marked and well-established road. The route laid out by Domingo Teran and Louis Juchereau Saint Denis in the late Seventeenth and early Eighteenth Centuries was still the only known, frequented, and practical road into Texas from east of the Sabine River. To the south was the "Big thicket," a densely wooded area thickly covered with underbrush that presented an almost impenetrable barrier to travel. Where the country was open pine woods and unfordable streams offered yet another barrier.

EARLY EAST TEXAS

On the north and west were Indian tribes who resented the white man's intrusion. The Cherokees and their related tribes occupied the area between the Trinity and the Sabine Rivers north of the King's Highway. West of them were the Waco, Tonkawas, and other tribes who were frequently predatory and sometimes hostile.

The traveler entering Texas through this well-known gateway found himself at once in a land of natural beauty and fertility in the red land belt that ran east and west along the path of the old road to San Antonio. It was a region situated between vast pine forests to the north and south composed of rolling hills and valleys covered with hardwoods and watered by clear streams of running water. The soil was deep red in color where it was exposed to view. Wildlife was abundant: deer, wild turkeys, squirrels, and game birds. Such a country attracted and held people who saw it, and many went no further into Texas.

Another attraction was the fact that all along the way from the Sabine to the Angelina Rivers these new arrivals encountered the remains of previous settlement. There were cleared fields and stock farms, remains of former dwellings, and a few of the older inhabitants. The unsettled conditions in East Texas from the times of the filibustering expeditions to the more recent Fredonian uprising had caused many early settlers to abandon their farms and ranches for more tranquil sites elsewhere.

There were, however, some signs of life along the Ayish Bayou. Taken together signs of previous settlement and a few residents contributed greatly to the rapid growth of settlement on the Red Lands, and the prominence which the Ayish Bayou District, as it came to be known, assumed in the affairs of East Texas. It sat astride the gateway to overland travel to Texas and welcomed all who passed its way.

In February 1821, records indicate that there were at least sixteen males living east of the Attoyac River in Texas, while three years later a petition contained thirty-six signatures. Another petition drafted about the same time states that there were more than 1,000 people settled between the eastern boundary of Texas and the Attoyac River.

The first great infiltration of immigrants to the area came following news of the Mexican Colonization Law of 1824. They hailed the liberal terms of this statute, but most found only after entering Texas that they would be forced to wait many years before they could benefit from its generous terms. In any event, by 1835 there were some 2,500 people living in the San Augustine Municipality which included settlements in Sabine and Shelby Counties as well as San Augustine County itself.

The early settlers in the Red Lands all, or nearly all, settled in the redland belt on either side of the main road that later was designated El Camino Real (the King's Highway). This old road at first only a mule trail was soon extended to San Antonio. As settlement expanded more and more immigrants located along the various water courses: Ayish Bayou, Palo Gacho, Patroon Creek, and Ironosa. The main body of settlers, however, were rather evenly distributed along the redlands, a strip about ten miles wide running east and west through the region

Mills and gins furnished meeting places as did county stores and a saloon or two. There were no churches because the people were predominately Protestants, and the Protestant religion was prohibited by Mexican law. But, in the end, the greatest amount of social intercourse was from farm to farm, as neighbors stopped in passing or visited in leisure times.

This scattering of settlements ultimately became known as the Ayish Bayou District, gaining its name from the fact that the stream of that name runs north to south through it. It included the settlements in the northern half of today's San Augustine County, together with those down the Attoyac River and a few along the Angelina River, the northern part of Sabine County and the eastern part of Shelby County, which was even then beginning to be known as the Tenahaw District. It was legally a part of the Municipality of Nacogdoches, but was regarded as a separate district because of the distance and because nearly all of its inhabitants were Anglo Americans, while the majority in Nacogdoches County were Mexicans.

It had no definite boundaries except the Attoyac was tacitly considered as one, and as a district had no standing in Mexican law. The commandant in Nacogdoches legally had jurisdiction, but fact he rarely interfered either for protection or for discipline. Moreover, the civil authorities in Nacogdoches never interfered except in the case of validating the occasional land grant. One cause of the neglect was almost certainly that all settlement there was in the area prohibited by the 1824 Colonization Law. Finally, Mexican authorities had little means or opportunity to attend to settlements so far distant from the seat of government.

Civil Government for San Augustine

Although they were nominally under the jurisdiction of the government of the Republic of Mexico, the settlers here between the Sabine and the Attoyac Rivers were forced by circumstances to create a body of laws and institutions of local government for themselves. They particularly needed a court of some kind to settle disputes that arose and to punish offenders against the public order. Acting on the suggestion of a Mexican officer, citizens of the area held a mass meeting and selected one of their number to preside over a common court and another to execute its decisions. The officer who presided over the court was called an alcalde after the Spanish-Mexican practice, while the other officers was called the sheriff after the old English practice. These two officers continued to be selected on an annual basis until 1833 when the Municipality of San Augustine was established. At that time three regidores or town councilors were added along with a sindico (town clerk) and other officers.

    The alcalde combined the functions of a County and District Judge who heard all cases and from whose decisions there was no appeal. The alcalde was authorized to summon a twelve-man jury to assist him in arriving at a decision. Since no one knew the provisions of Spanish law verdicts were rendered "according to the evidence and the rights of the case." The only written laws administered by alcalde and sheriff were a set of rules and regulations drawn up at the original mass meeting and corresponding so far as the settlers knew to Mexican law.

    The character of the settlers themselves is demonstrated by the fact that under these rather primitive conditions they went ahead with their ordinary day-to-day affairs, bought and sold, bartered and traded, contracted and collected debts, and conducted the traditional business of the community. The people were not vexed by taxes of any kind, customs duties were not levied and collected, nor were any sorts of licenses required. Newcomers settled on land they freely chose, provided it was not already occupied, built their homes, cleared their farms, planted their crops and prospered according to their ability. The alcaldes elected in these early years included Nathan Davis, Bailey Anderson, John Sprowl, Jacob Garrett, and Elisha Roberts. Early sheriffs were George English and Alexander Horton.

At last, on March 6, 1834, the old extra-legal District of Ayish Bayou disappeared and was replaced by the Municipality of San Augustine. Its limits were described as beginning at the junction of Little Cow Creek and the Sabine River, thence in a straight line to the mouth of the Ayish Bayou, ascending the Attoyac River to its principal headwaters, thence north to the Sabine River, descending it to the place of beginning. With those boundaries it included all of San Augustine, Sabine, and Shelby Counties, more than half of Panola County, the northern section of Newton County, and a small part of Jasper County. It was given the name San Augustine after the famous Roman Catholic Bishop of Hippo in the fourth century.

Thus, forty years after the inhabitants of the

region began to petition for titles to their land they and their territory received official recognition by the Mexican government. Provoked by long and causeless delays, they had joined rebellion after rebellion. New waves of immigrants had come in and Spanish rule overturned, but their condition had not improved. Not until the shadows of a coming revolution appeared were their demands granted.

The Municipality of Nacogdoches

For centuries Nacogdoches had been the focal point for settlement in East Texas. At the confluence of the Banita and La Nana Creeks, the site had been initially a Caddo village, the location of a Spanish mission and garrison, a frontier outpost, and a Mexican municipality. Its population reduced to less than one hundred in 1821 as a result of filibustering expeditions and further depleted by the short-lived Fredonian Rebellion, the settlement thereafter slowly began to recover. Many of those who fled in 1826 began slowly and quietly to return, and the growing influx of Anglo Americans added to their numbers. By 1828 it had grown to approximately 1,000 and steadily increased thereafter.

At the end of the Fredonian Rebellion an ayuntamiento (town council) was created to assist the alcalde, varying with the years from three to five members. The municipal government also included a sindico (secretary), regidores (advisors), and a sindico procurador (attorney). All elected officials held office for a period of one year.

Municipal officials faced vexing problems during these years as a Mexican government. Since El Camino Real (the Royal Road) traversed the center of the town, and since Nacogdoches was a "Gateway to Texas," large number of immigrants passed through on their way to empresario grants and other areas in the interior of the province. Its location near the border of the United States and Mexico was also a source of trouble. Hence many of the regulations laid down by the ayuntamiento were designed to establish and maintain law and order in a frontier town.

But, in addition, the local officials attempted to make Nacogdoches an attractive place for immigrants to become permanent residents. They laid out streets according to a plan provided by the central government for all Spanish colonial towns in the New World. This plan called for a series of plazas or squares with streets straightened and widened to twenty varas (about fifty-five feet) leading away at each of the four corners. A Plaza Principal for government buildings and a religious plaza were two examples. Space was reserved on the Church Plaza for a town hall, jail, and school. A public water well was dug in the center of the Plaza Principal to provide water for residents and travelers and the church cemetery enclosed with a picket fence.

After order had been restored following the Fredonian Rebellion, a Mexican garrison composed of Colonel José las Piedras and the Twelfth Battalion was stationed in Nacogdoches, Samuel Norris was reinstated as alcalde, and a general amnesty was proclaimed for participants in the Fredonian Rebellion, with exception of Haden and Benjamin Edwards, Martin Parmer, and Adolphus Sterne, a local merchant. Sterne, a native of Germany, had commercial contacts, and it was an easy matter for him to obtain supplies for the rebels.

The religious life of the community began to be altered. The buildings of the old Mission Guadalupe were abandoned after having been used as a chapel by the local Spanish garrison and local Catholics and a new parish church built on Church Plaza on present day North Street. This building was also abandoned during the Mexican Revolution and in time was used as a barracks for the Twelfth Battalion.

Manuel de Mier y Terán, Commandant of the Eastern Province of Texas, visited East Texas in 1828. He reported that Nacogdoches was a town of some 700 inhabitants of whom only some 100 were female. The buildings were constructed of wood, except for the Stone House with crooked streets that remained at the mercy of the weather. Local government functioned in its usual irascible way constantly concerned with matters of public order, health, and commerce.

Terán was disturbed by signs of abuse at the garrison: the men had gone unpaid for months and their supplies were nearly exhausted. As elsewhere in Texas, he saw that the Mexican population seemed relegated to lesser positions, none owned a mercantile establishment, and few occupied professional status. But perhaps most disturbing was the flood tide of Anglo American immigration.

Perhaps the most pressing problem facing Colonel Piedras and the local civil government after 1826 was the illegal entry of foreigners (generally Anglo Americans) into Texas. The Mexican colonel received repeated complaints from alcaldes throughout the Nacogdoches District concerning the steady infiltration of aliens and their stubborn refusal to obtain legal permission to become permanent settlers. In characteristic Anglo American fashion they questioned and resented the authority of the Mexican government or any government to tell them where they could settle.

Colonel Piedras publicly declared that he did not possess the necessary manpower to prevent immigrants from bypassing him and his garrison. By 1830 the volume of immigrants streaming into Texas from the U. S. caused Mexican authorities to see them as a threat to their continued control over the area. As a consequence, on April 6 the National Congress in Mexico City decreed that citizens of foreign countries adjacent to Mexican territory could no longer enter and settle in Texas closing the door to further Anglo American immigration.

This action of the Mexican government came as a shock to the Anglo Americans who had already taken up residence in Texas and who expected still more of their fellows to join them. Many of them reacted by losing faith in the integrity of the governor of the new Mexican nation. Their vision of a Texas as a haven for Anglo American settlement seemed lost.

The Town of San Augustine

Near the end of this rather brief period of peace and tranquility, the resident of the old Ayish Bayou settlement now known as the Municipality of San Augustine began to sense the need for a permanent location for the administration of the public affairs of the community. For example, for some time the alcalde's court was regularly held at the home of the alcalde which meant that when a new judge was selected the court moved to a different location. This annual shifting of the court's place soon became extremely inconvenient as the population of the district began to increase and the court's business increased in volume. Moreover, a private residence, often a small one of perhaps two rooms and a "dog trot," was inadequate to accommodate the business of a court. Public records needed to be kept at some site readily accessible to all citizens. Other factors also contributed, such as the need for a central market place for trade and commerce.

Thus at some time in 1832, perhaps on the eve of the next outbreak of rebellion in East Texas, at a mass meeting of the people of the municipality support was forthcoming for the project of building a town to meet those needs. A committee of fifteen men was selected to select the site. They examined several localities and ultimately decided that the place should be between the Ayish Bayou and the Carizzo Creek on the east side of the Bayou. They had determined that the projected town should be located at some central spot along the main road through the Red Lands. The spot selected had once been the site of a permanent Indian village and an early Spanish mission.

The land on which the town would be built was a part of the four league grant of Edmund Quirk of which two square miles had been sold to Chichester Chaplin. From this parcel Chaplin sold 640 acres to Thomas S. McFarland on the east side of the Bayou. It was bounded on the west by the Bayou and on the south by the King's Highway and contained the old mission site.

EARLY EAST TEXAS

Thomas McFarland was commissioned to survey the land, lay out the town, and sell the lots. The town site lay on the eastern bank of the Ayish Bayou and on either side of the main road. It was composed of forty-eight blocks divided into 356 lots with streets forty feet wide. Two lots near the center were reserved for a public square on which a courthouse was later erected. Contrary to the plan prescribed by Spanish-Mexican law and custom, the town was laid out on the American grid plan.

During the town's early history the only municipal building was the custom house where duties were collected on goods coming in from the United States. San Augustine, at the time, was the third most important port of entry with only Galveston and Matagorda ranking above her. After Texas Independence this building was also used as a courthouse.

The 1830 decree prohibiting further colonization by Anglo Americans also imposed customs duties and the machinery for collecting them and provided for the garrisoning of troops in Texas towns. Out of this action grew a chain of events that led inexorably to armed conflict. By this legislation Mexican authorities demonstrated clearly that they intended to bring Texas under national control and to integrate the frontier province on wholly Mexican terms. Legally Mexico had every right to attempt this

EARLY EAST TEXAS

feat, but the East Texas colonists, in turn, believed that they had a moral right to resist.

Those settlers along with most other Anglo American in Texas regarded the 1830 law as calamity. In their view the colony was beginning to grow and prosper. This growth was based, they contended, on immigration. Immigration meant more towns, thirteen had already been established, all predominantly Anglo American. This meant more stores, more cotton gins, and more commerce in general. The end of Anglo American immigration would bring stagnation. Perhaps worst of all, they regarded the decrees as a gratuitous insult to them and their kind.

In the older more settled parts of Mexico a military dictatorship was rapidly developing. The nation soon collapsed into political anarchy with military rule imposed everywhere by garrisons. In the process twelve garrisons were created in Texas. The freedom-loving Anglo Americans in Texas resented the imposition of military rule. The Mexican commanders were imperious dons, and the ranks were drawn from the lowest classes south of the Rio Grande.

As a result, meetings were called and strong protests issued. As could readily be expected Mexican authorities from San Antonio to Mexico City saw these actions as seditious, since peaceful assembly had never been a Mexican custom. Insurrection and open

EARLY EAST TEXAS

revolt was in the offing.

EARLY EAST TEXAS

CHAPTER FIVE

THE BATTLE OF NACOGDOCHES

In East Texas as tensions mounted, an event occurred in 1832 that had a far-reaching effect on the history of Texas. An open revolt against the authority of the Mexican government was launched which marked the end of the era of Mexican rule in the town and throughout the region.

In East Texas and especially in Nacogdoches the causes of the clash between Mexican authority and Anglo American resistance were reasonably complex. Initially, they grew out of the people's grievances against Colonel Piedras, the Nacogdoches commandant, because of his fears that he would face armed defiance of his authority. As early as 1828 complaints of false arrest, brutality, misappropriation of funds, cattle theft, and failure to pay his debts were voiced against the commandant.

But it was the Immigration Law of 1830 which most outraged the Nacogdoches area settlers. Although Juan Antonio Padilla, Commissioner of Land Titles in East Texas, was reluctant to enforce the law, his arrest on murder charges brought the business of granting land titles to a standstill and firmly convinced the Anglo Americans that the Mexicans

EARLY EAST TEXAS

were conspiring against them.

In defense of Colonel Piedras, it is quite clear that his position was precarious and uncomfortable. In the discharge of his duties, he received little cooperation from the local ayuntamiento and other local officials. The soldiers under his command did not inspire confidence, their exposed situation few in number and far from any sort of reinforcements, and the growing ill temper of the local population combined to make his despair of maintaining Mexican control over East Texas. He was sure that the steady influx of foreigners who were often insolent and scornful would welcome an opportunity to separate Texas from Mexico.

The Battle Erupts

The summer of 1832 brought on the impending crisis. In June Piedras and fifty men of his command rushed to Anahuac to help put down a disturbance brought about by the arrest of William B. Travis and Patrick Jack. Realizing that he could expect little help from Mexican authorities in San Antonio and beyond and wishing to avoid if possible a repeat of the Anahuac disturbances, the Mexican colonel determined to confiscate the people's firearms. This action so alarmed the local people that on July 28 the Nacogdoches ayuntamiento called upon the neighboring settlements to join them in resisting the attempt to disarm them.

When copies of the Nacogdoches resolution reached the surrounding settlements, all responded except San Felipe in Austin's colony. Companies of volunteers commanded by Captains Bailey Anderson, Isaac W. Burton, Vicente Cordova, Wyatt Hanks, and Frederick Moz from San Augustine, Sabine, Teneha, and Bevil were joined to form the "National Militia" under the command of Colonel James Whitis Bullock of San Augustine. An additional company commanded by Captain James Bradshaw came from the Neches settlements also joined the group.

Realizing that an attack was imminent, Colonel Piedras called for instructions and reinforcements from San Antonio. He also realized that if help was sent it might well be too late in arriving. Nacogdoches merchants had boarded up their stores and removed their goods to safety, leaving the garrison without supplies.

August 2, 1832, the Mexican colonel's worst fears were realized. That morning the armed settlers massed on Pine Hill about a mile east of Nacogdoches, elected Colonel Bullock their commander, and sent Piedras an ultimatum. He was to declare in favor of General Antonio L. Santa Anna and the Constitution of 1824 or surrender within four hours. Piedras reject both alternatives. Instead he invited them to meet with him, saying he would be glad to receive them and open discussions.

Shortly before noon the armed settlers began an advance toward the town, and Piedras' troops withdrew to the Stone House, the church, and the Red House. Eschewing a frontal attack down the town's main street, the insurgents made their way around the town to the east and north to gain the Mexicans' rear. They then marched down what today is known as North Street, and in the vicinity of the Church Plaza diverged to their left where under cover of a ravine they advanced toward the Stone House where they were met by a cavalry charge on their right and a volley of musket fire on their left.

The cavalry charge initially disorganized the settlers, but they soon regrouped and began a house-to-house fight. In the mid-afternoon the Mexicans were forced out of the Stone House and took refuge nearby in the Red House, Piedras' headquarters. Firing ceased when darkness fell.

During the nighttime hours the townspeople constructed breastworks and other fortifications expecting the battle to continue the next morning. They were quite surprised when at dawn a reconnaissance revealed no one stirring except the parish priest who informed the settlers that Piedras and his men had fled during the night leaving only their dead and wounded behind. Whereupon some of them knocked down the door to the Red House and finding no one there, set out in pursuit of the Mexican troops.

Later on the John Durst Road about seven miles east of the Angelina River, they encountered the rear guard of Piedras' troops and commenced firing on the Mexicans. Piedras halted and formed his men for action, but the rather small group of pursuers broke off and retreated. Thereafter the Americans changed their position, moved around behind the Mexicans, and set up an ambush at Durst's Ferry on the Angelina River. When an advanced guard of three calvary men stopped at the river to water their horses, they were immediately shot.

When Colonel Piedras heard the firing, he began organizing his troops for battle. He formed them in platoons close to the river and launched an attack against the Americans. The Americans thereupon opened fire and made the Mexican advance give way. The same result occurred for four more Mexican attacks, whereupon Piedras retreated to John Durst's home on the river. Nightfall prevented the Americans from pursuing them.

During the night Mrs. Durst sent her son to the American camp with information that Piedras was willing to surrender. Approaching the house early the following morning, the settlers saw a white flag waving from a window. The Mexican colonel and his officers were returned to Nacogdoches while the remainder of his force was held at the river.

The surrender terms agreed upon by Piedras and his captors called for John Durst to take charge of the troops and march them westward to San Antonio. Piedras and his officers, however, would be returned to Mexico City on shipboard by way of New Orleans. Jim Bowie, who later to became a hero of the Texas Revolution, had arrived in Nacogdoches a few days after the battle agreed to convey the Mexican troops to San Antonio while Piedras and his officers were taken to Velasco by Asa N. Edwards.

Mexican casualties numbered thirty-three killed, and seventeen or eighteen wounded. The Americans suffered only three dead and seven wounded. Unfortunately, one of the dead was Encarnacion Chireno, the Nacogdoches alcalde.

The Battle of Nacogdoches has been referred to as the "opening gun of the Texas Revolution" because as a result, no Mexican troops remained in Texas east of San Antonio. This condition allowed the Consultations of 1832, 1833, and 1835 as well as the Convention at Washington-on-the-Brazos in 1836, to meet without threat of military intervention and prevented Sam Houston's troops from fearing an attack from their rear at San Jacinto.

One of the most intriguing legends of East Texas history relates to an episode growing out of the

EARLY EAST TEXAS

battle. As the story is usually told, Colonel Piedras enlisted the service of a blacksmith, William Goyens, "a free man of color" as he was legally designated. Goyens, a native of North Carolina, immigrated to Texas in 1820 where he soon became the principal craftsman in the Nacogdoches area. He was commissioned by the Mexican colonel to forge two large cans out of two large copper pots furnished by Piedras. When Goyens had finished the task, he was dismissed but told to return the following day. At that time, the colonel ordered him to seal the cans without examining their contents.

Although the blacksmith did not inspect the contents, he was convinced that one of them contained gold coins and the other jewels and valuables from the local Catholic Church. When the lids had been soldered, Piedras ordered them buried west of town somewhere along the banks of Ysletta Creek. When he and his troops were defeated and withdrew from the town, the Mexican officer did not get an opportunity to retrieve the treasure. Since that time, treasure hunters have searched but have failed to locate the legendary treasure trove.

Just prior to the battle, in 1831 the Department of Nacogdoches was created out of the old Department of Bexar. From that time down to the Texas Revolution in 1836, the Department of Nacogdoches included all of Texas east of the Trinity

EARLY EAST TEXAS

River. After the battle, Nacogdoches experienced a brief period of tranquility. It population quietly increased to the point that in 1835 there were more than 3,500 inhabitants.

Elsewhere in East Texas

The Mexican restriction prohibiting settlements within twenty leagues of the boundary curtailed legitimate settlement in the area immediately west of the Sabine River. As a consequence, the strip attracted persons given to violence and lawlessness and discouraged permanent residents. The territory in the northern section of the Nacogdoches Municipality was organized as the Tenaha (Teneja, Tenaha, Teneha) District in 1827 by Nathan Davis with Nashville (now Shelbyville) as its principal settlement. It included territory now included within the present counties of Shelby, Panola, Harrison, Rusk, Upshur, and Marion Counties.

In 1835 this region was organized as the Tenahaw Municipality with Nashville as the seat of its government. The following year the name of the Municipality was changed to Shelby to honor Isaac Shelby, an American Revolutionary soldier from Tennessee. By 1837 Nashville had been renamed Shelbyville when the area was organized as a American style county. It remained the seat of

EARLY EAST TEXAS

government until 1866 when the county seat was moved to Center.

Most Anglo American settlers came from the states of the Old South and brought with them the institution of slavery. Thereafter, slaves made up a substantial portion of the population. In 1847, 763 slaves made up about twenty-three percent of the 3,318 residents; and in 1860, 1,476 of 5,362 or twenty-seven percent.

After 1837 when county government was instituted, land titles were issued to anyone who settled on a tract of unoccupied land and asked for legal title. Overlapping land claims understandably created friction between settlers. Disputes over land ownership and the absence of a strong law enforcement machinery ultimately led to a three-year period of violence known as the Regulator-Moderator War. During this time individual persons were killed or tried and hanged, the county's economy was devastated, land values plummeted, and the flow of immigration turned aside.

Meanwhile, Spanish activity which had begun in the southern portion of the Nacogdoches Municipality in 1716 when some sixty-five persons left San Antonio traveling some 400 miles to found a mission at a site four leagues (10.5 miles) further west than the old Tejas mission. Named Mission San Francisco de los Neches, it was located east of the

EARLY EAST TEXAS

Neches River, six miles from present day Alto in Cherokee County. In 1730 at the request of the missionaries, it was moved to the vicinity of Zilker Park on the Colorado River in Austin.

El Camino Real was the determining factor in the selection of land by the first settlers in the region. Land along its route contained the best soil in the Red Lands, and was along a well-traveled road. Early in the Eighteenth Century, Saint Denis had led an expedition into East Texas that took him through what is now northern Sabine County along the Old San Antonio Road, but it was not until late in the century that the Spanish began issuing land grants.

Jack Cedars, an Anglo male who married the daughter of the captain of the Spanish garrison at the Borreagas Crossing of Borreagas Creek in the northern part of the present-day Sabine County, was the first Anglo American settler. Prior to 1832 the region was a part of the Municipality of Nacogdoches, but from 1832 to 1835 a part of the Municipality of San Augustine, and it was not until 1835 that the Municipality of Sabine was established.

James Gaines, a native of Virginia, became the first alcalde of the Sabine District. He was a cousin of Lieutenant Edmund P. Gaines of the United States Army and in 1803 accompanied his relative in making a survey of the waterway from Nashville, Tennessee down the Cumberland River to the Ohio River then

EARLY EAST TEXAS

down the Ohio to Mississippi River on to New Orleans. In 1805, he went with the American troops to Fort Jessup near Natchitoches.

While there in 1812 Augustus Magee enlisted him with the rank of captain for service in the ill-fated Magee-Gutiérrez Expedition. He may have also been a participant in the Dr. James Long Expeditions.

In 1814, Gaines married Susanna Norris, a sister of Samuel Norris who became an alcalde in Nacogdoches. They soon established a home just across the Sabine River from the Neutral Strip. In time he acquired ownership of a ferry service and opened a tavern at what became known as Gaines Ferry. His ferry was situated at a major entry point for immigrants coming to Texas.

The Milam settlement was established in the northern section of the district along the King's Highway in 1828, and in 1858, it became the first county seat of Sabine County. However, the Geneva settlement originally known as Shawnee Village had grown up also in the northern section of the district. Many local historians believe that the village is the oldest continuously occupied pueblo in East Texas. By far the largest number of early Anglo Americans settlers entered Texas via the ferries across the Sabine River into the Sabine District. The earliest crossing employed by the Spanish was at a shoal in the river located above the Gaines Ferry crossing. The area around the Milam settlement was then called Las Boreagas by the Indians, but early settlers called it Red Mound. Thus, when the town of Milam was surveyed in 1828, it was named Red Mound, but the name was soon changed at the insistence of John S. Roberts to honor Texas hero Ben Milam. Milam thereafter for a time was the first town travelers encountered along El Camino Real. In 1839, the town of Sabine, known today as Sabinetown, with its ferry replaced Milam. The town soon became the largest village in the area having the advantage of a river port and being located on the Royal Road.

In 1837, Sabine County was organized and its boundaries defined. Its population in 1847 was 1,021, in 1850 it had grown to 2,498 of whom 942 were slaves.

In 1841, a Methodist Church bishop wrote a letter to his brother clergyman describing the land along this route. Leaving the river port he found the land level with sandy soil for some four miles but thereafter he encountered higher ground and the red lands. East of Milam the country, he reported, was "pleasant and plentiful" with excellent spring water in abundant quantities.

The southernmost portion of the original Municipality of Nacogdoches along the Neches River began to be settled by Europeans between 1800 and 1810. There they encountered Cherokee and Alabama

EARLY EAST TEXAS

and Cousatta Indians, the later recent immigrants from Louisiana. Those early settlers were predominantly from the American south, many of whom planned to resume the slave-holding society with which they were familiar. The forests and soil that was sandy loam, however, were not suited for growing cotton; so many of them left the area, but most of the ones who stayed were poor white farmers who owned no slaves. One of the first settlements in the region was known as Fort Terán and was located on the Neches River where it crossed the Old Spanish Trail from Nacogdoches to Liberty. Another early community was known as Town Bluff and served as the first seat of government for the area beginning in 1842. Three years later it was moved to Woodville. These settlements were organized as Tyler County in 1846 when its boundaries were defined. It was originally known as the Menard District of Liberty Municipality. Population of the area stood at 1,894 in 1850 and 4,525 in 1860 of whom some 1,175 were slaves.

  The Battle of Nacogdoches marked the beginning of the end for Nacogdoches as a Mexican town. Thereafter, the town's character became steadily more Anglo American. Other East Texas settlements to the north, east, and south of the old Spanish frontier post had for their origins been dominated by Anglo American elements.

  A brief period of tranquility in East Texas

EARLY EAST TEXAS

followed the Battle of Nacogdoches, but a chain of events that would lead to rebellion and independence in four short years had begun to be forged. What was developing was a deep-seated cultural conflict, in which Anglos and Mexicans clashed again and again. Mexicans failed to comprehend or understand the fact that as frontier Anglo Americans the Anglo Texans were content only so long as they were left virtually free from governmental interference in their lives.

EARLY EAST TEXAS

CHAPTER SIX

REVOLUTION AND AFTER

In the years immediately following the Law of 1830, the Mexican government sought to "maintain the integrity of its territory" by first sending a customs collector to Texas and following him more soldiers to enforce the laws of the nation. The new customs inspector for ports east of the Colorado River was George Fisher, a native of Hungary and a Mexican national for less than ten years; and John Davis Bradburn, a stubborn, tactless Kentucky native, who had entered Mexican civil service in 1817, was given the important post as collector at Anahuac at the head of Galveston Bay.

With Mexican troops at his command, Bradburn decreed that shipmasters who wished to leave Texas from the mouth of the Brazos River and other nearby ports to were to secure clearances from him at Anahuac before sailing. Since this required of some that they undertake a two hundred mile journey, some captains ignored the order and ran by the fort on the lower Brazos.

Bradburn's decree was soon countermanded by his superiors and new deputy collectors located at Brazoria on the lower reaches of the river. This did not satisfy the colonists who were reluctant to pay customs duties no matter how convenient. They had been exempt too long to relish a new system of taxes.

Colonel Bradburn soon further provoked bitter resentment. First, he arrested, in early 1831, Francisco Madero, who had come to Texas with authority to grant land titles to settlers living east of the San Jacinto River. Many of those people had been in Texas many years and had waited for years for legal ownership of their land. Thereafter, Bradburn dissolved for a time the ayuntamiento of Liberty that Madero had installed.

In addition, settlers charged the Mexican colonel with encouraging slaves to run away and refusing to deliver them to their owners on demand. They also alleged that he extorted supplies for his garrison, used slave labor on public works without compensating their owners, and refused to punish soldiers for offenses against civilians. For their deliberate disregard of his authority, Bradburn arrested William B. Travis and Patrick Jack.[5] They were lodged in an old brick kiln an he refused to

---

[5] Travis was a South Carolina lawyer who had abandoned his wife and family and immigrated to Texas in 1831. Jack was a Georgia lawyer and veteran of the War of 1812 who arrived in Texas in 1830.

EARLY EAST TEXAS

deliver them up to civil authorities for trial.

The prolonged imprisonment of the two young lawyers prompted colonial resistance. William H. Jack, Patrick's brother, tried without success to secure their release. Whereupon he returned to San Felipe and called on his fellow colonists to join him in an attack on Bradburn. Colonial forces numbering some 160 men appeared before Anahuac but withdrew to await the arrival of cannon from Brazoria.

Colonel Piedras, commandant of the Nacogdoches garrison soon arrived with a portion of his troops and orders to mediate the matter. He entered into an agreement with the colonists that called for release of Travis and Jack to civil authorities, payment for the property that Bradburn had seized, and removal of Bradburn from his post. Bradburn soon resigned, and the garrison declared for General Santa Anna and sailed away to join his forces.

Although the quarrel at Anahuac was resolved with little bloodshed, further conflict was brewing. The San Felipe forces set out for Brazoria where they secured three cannon and prepared to take them to Anahuac, but the Mexican commandant at Velasco four miles from the mouth of the Brazos River would not permit the schooner to pass his fort. A bloody engagement ensued ending with the surrender of the fort. Once launched at Velasco the resistance movement spread and Anglo Texans determined to drive every Mexican soldier from the nearby settlements. In a short while the Anglo American part of Texas was completely rid of Mexican soldiers.

Conventions in 1832 and 1833

The insurrection of 1832 resulted in the expulsion of Mexican troops and the suspension of customs duties and the blessing of General Santa Anna. Not willing to leave matters as they stood, the colonists demanded a constructive reform program. Accordingly, in August the ayuntamiento of San Felipe issued a call for a meeting of delegates in October at San Felipe to formulate their demands. Fifty-eight delegates from sixteen districts assembled to answer the call. Charles S. Taylor, Thomas Hastings, and Hyman Hertz represented the Nacogdoches District[6]; Benjamin Holt, and Jesse

---

[6] Taylor was a native of England who arrived in Nacogdoches in 1828. He soon entered the mercantile business as a sole proprietor but later in partnership with Charles H. Simms and still later with Adolphus Sterne. Hastings, a native of New York, who came to Nacogdoches early in the 1820s and also engaged in the mercantile business. Hertz came to Nacogdoches from his native Germany in 1829. Twenty-one

EARLY EAST TEXAS

Parker the Sabine District[7]; Phillip A. Sublett, Donald McDonald, William McFarland, Wyatt Hanks, and Jacob Garrett the Ayish Bayou (San Augustine) District[8]; William English, Frederick Foye, George

---

years old and single, he soon entered the mercantile business.

    [7] Holt was born about 1798 in North Carolina who was living in Nacogdoches by 1834. He was a farmer and later was a county officer in Angelina County. Parker had been born in North Carolina about 1797 and came to Texas in 1822. He served as Deputy Land commissioner for Montgomery County in 1834.

    [8] Sublett immigrated from his native Kentucky in 1824 and married a daughter of Elisha Roberts. He was chairman of the Committee of Safety and Correspondence in 1835 and an officer in Houston's Army. McDonald was born in Canada in 1789 and a veteran of the British army in the War of 1812. He settled in southwestern San Augustine County and entered partnership with Wyatt Hanks in a sawmill and was a sometime ferryman. McFarland was born in Lancaster, Pennsylvania in 1774. He was a surveyor, soldier, and public servant who came to Texas in 1830. Hanks was a miller and farmer who came to Texas from Indiana

EARLY EAST TEXAS

Butler, John M. Bradley, and Jonas Harrison the Tenehaw (Shelby) District[9]; and Thomas D. Beauchamp, Elijah Isaacs, Samuel Loony and James

---

County, Kentucky. He was a member of the General Council in the Provisional Government. Garrett was born about 1776 in Tennessee and came to Texas in 1824 from Arkansas. He was chosen alcalde of the San Augustine District.

[9] English, a native of New River, Virginia, was born there about 1790. He came to Texas in 1825 where he participated in the Fredonian Rebellion and served as a member of the legislature of Coahuila y Texas. He was a farmer and stockman. Foye came to Texas "before 1835" and in censuses was listed as a farmer and stockman. Butler was a native of Georgia who came to Texas by 1832. He was a justice of the peace and Associate Land Commissioner. Bradley was a member of Stephen F. Austin's "Old Three Hundred," who settled in the Ayish Bayou District by 1832, participated in the Fredonian Rebellion, and raised a volunteer company for the Texas Revolution. Harrison was born in Woodbridge Township, New Jersey in 1777. He was a distinguished lawyer who immigrated to Texas in 1820. He served as alcalde of the Tenaha District and later practiced law in Nacogdoches.

EARLY EAST TEXAS

Loony the Neches (Tyler County) District[10]. McFarland, Harrison, and Taylor all "solid, substantial, conservative men who had been active in Ayish Bayou affairs became leaders.

    The delegates assured the Mexicans of their unqualified support for the federation and its constitution. They asked that the State of Coahuila y Texas supply land titles to settlers east of Austin's colony, that additional ayuntamientos be established there, and that the state set aside land for school purposes. They also asked that the federal government exempt them from customs duties on necessities for three years, and that customs officials be appointed by local alcaldes. Further, they approved a plan for organizing the local militia and recommended plans for common defense against the Indians.

    Delegates indicated that two of their requests took precedence over all others: repeal of the prohibition against further Anglo American immigration, and separation from Coahuila and

---

[10] Beauchamp came to Texas in 1832. Isaacs was born in 1775 in North Carolina and came to Texas from Pike County, Mississippi in 1822. Samuel Loony was a major in the Texas Army during the Revolution. James Loony came to Texas from Kentucky in 1828. He had been born about 1800.

EARLY EAST TEXAS

statehood for Texas. For unknown reasons these petitions for redress of grievances were never presented to either state or federal governments.

Expressions of disapproval from Mexican authorities prompted the call for a second convention to meet at San Felipe on April 1 the next year. For this meeting districts represented were the same as the first. Adolphus Sterne, Thomas Hastings, and Sam Houston were representatives from the Nacogdoches District[11]. John English represented the Tenaha or Shelby District,[12] while the Sabine District apparently sent no representatives. The San Augustine District

---

[11] Sterne was born in 1801 in Cologne, Germany. At age sixteen he left home going first to New Orleans and in 1826 to Texas. He participated in the Fredonian Rebellion, and in later years he served as alcalde of the Nacogdoches Municipality, as a member of its ayuntamiento, and as its Primary Judge. In 1836 in New Orleans he recruited and outfitted two companies of troops known as the New Orleans Greys.

[12] English was a native of Virginia having been born there in 1793. He fought in the War of 1812. He immigrated to Texas in 1825 and participated in the Texas Revolution. His occupation was listed a farmer.

EARLY EAST TEXAS

sent Archilles Edmund Challis Johnson, Elisha Roberts, and Phillip Sublett.[13] Only about a third of the delegates who attended the 1833 assembly had attended the 1832 Consultation.

The petitions addressed to state and federal governments featured the same grievances set forth in those of the 1832 delegates. Again emphasis was placed on the repeal of the anti-immigration law of 1830 and separation of Texas from the State of Coahuila. Acting on the assumption that their request for separate statehood would be approved, the 1833 delegates drafted a state constitution for the Mexican state of Texas. To no one's surprise the proposed constitution was typically Anglo American in all important features.

In the Conventions of 1832 and 1833, the San Augustine and Nacogdoches delegates played prominent parts. Charles S. Taylor's committee

---

[13] Johnson was a native of Virginia who came to Texas from Missouri about 1824. He was a member of the committee to select a site for the town of San Augustine. Roberts was born near Nashville, Tennessee in 1774. He immigrated first to Kentucky, then to Louisiana before coming to Texas in 1824. He early established a cotton gin in the Ayish Bayou settlement. He was elected alcalde of San Augustine in 1831.

drafted the proposals adopted for dealing with the Cherokees and other Indians to the north. William McFarland's committee led the movement for a declaration of independence which was supported strongly by Jonas Harrison. Sam Houston's committee drafted the constitution that was ultimately adopted.

Confident of approval of their requests, the delegates prevailed on Stephen F. Austin to journey to Mexico City to present their petitions. As a result of a series of misunderstandings and Austin's impatience of delays, the Texan was arrested at Saltillo on his way home from Mexico City and returned to the Mexican capital where he was lodged in the Prison of the Inquisition. The intervention of two attorneys: Peter W. Grayson and Spencer H. Jack, and petitions from Texas seeking his discharge succeeded in securing his release on bail in late 1834, but not until an amnesty law was enacted in mid-July 1835 was he allowed to return to Texas.

The Consultation of 1835 and The Convention of 1836

In the months following the adjournment of the 1833 Convention a relative calm settled over the province. This state of affairs was produced by several important factors. There was widespread satisfaction with the work of the 1833 meeting. Moreover, a series of natural disasters focused the settler's attention on survival rather than political activity. An outbreak of floods, a cholera epidemic, and the onset of bouts of malignant malaria caught and held their attention. As a result, in 1833 and 1834 the Anglo Texans adopted a policy of watchful waiting.

During those two years the state government was generous in responding to the grievances of the Texans. Its legislature repealed the law that prohibited all but native-born Mexican nationals from engaging in retail merchandising, divided the province into three political departments with their seats of government at San Antonio, San Felipe, and Nacogdoches, representation in the state legislature was increased to three of the twelve deputies, English was recognized as an official language, and religious toleration was granted. Moreover, the court system was reorganized with a superior court created for Texas and trial by jury initiated.

Texans slowly became divided into three political factions: a small but active war party, a small, active, and persistent peace party, and the great majority of settlers who adopted a neutral position. Their indifference early gradually became more untenable as the currents of revolution gathered momentum. Events during 1835 favored the agenda of the war party.

Stephen F. Austin returned to Texas in

EARLY EAST TEXAS

September, 1835, convinced that Texans could not expect to achieve their goals because political turmoil in Mexico centered around the actions of General Santa Anna and unwise land laws enacted by the state government prevented their achievement. Santa Anna had become a virtual dictator after dissolving the national and state legislatures and wrecking the federal system of government. Texans feared the onset of military rule, a condition totally unacceptable to freedom-loving Anglo Americans.

Moreover, they bitterly resented state land laws that permitted what they perceived as unwise and dishonest land sales. An 1834 statute authorized the state governor to dispose of as much as 400 leagues (1,771,200 acres) of land to maintain the militia in providing defense against the Indians. An 1835 law empowered the governor to dispose of an additional 400 leagues with absolute authority to determine the methods of disposal and the use of the proceeds. A second 1835 enactment allowed the governor to grant several hundred additional leagues to land speculators.

Consequently, on August 15, 1835, a committee of fifteen men chosen by a group of citizens meeting at Columbia issued an urgent call for a convention or consultation. They suggested that each Texas district to elect five delegates to meet on October 15 at Washington-on-the-Brazos. Texans responded to the call by choosing fifty-five delegates, representing some thirteen municipalities.

The Nacogdoches Municipality actually elected six delegates: David Hoffman, Daniel Parker, Nathan Robbins, James W. Robinson, Thomas J. Rusk, and William Whitaker.[14] Representatives of the San Augustine Municipality were Henry W. Augustine, Jacob Garrett, Alexander Horton, Almanson Huston, Archilles Edmond Challis Johnson, Albert G. Kellog, and William N. Sigler[15]

---

[14] Hoffman came to Texas in 1832 and was immediately selected as a member of the committee to locate the site of the town of San Augustine. He later operated a merchandise business in Nacogdoches where he served a short term as alcalde. Parker was a pioneer Baptist minister who had been born in Virginia in 1781. He immigrated first to Illinois and in 1833 to Texas bringing his church with him. Robbins came to Texas in 1828 settling on Bidais Creek where the King's Highway crossed the Trinity River. There he operated a ferry for many years. Whitaker came to Texas from Louisiana in 1822. He listed his occupation as farmer.

[15] Augustine immigrated from Watauga County, Alabama in 1827. He participated in the Battle of Nacogdoches. He had been born about 1795. Horton was born in 1810 in

EARLY EAST TEXAS

Branch T. Archer,[16] delegate from the District of Columbia, was elected to preside over the assembly. He quickly appointed John A. Wharton[17],

---

Halifax County, North Carolina. He came to Texas with his brother in 1824 locating on the Attoyac River along the King's Highway. He participated in the Battle of Nacogdoches. From 1831 to 1833 he was sheriff of the Ayish Bayou District. He also participated in the Battle of San Jacinto. Huston was born in New York in 1799. He came to Texas by 1829 in time to participate in the Texas Revolution. Kellog was a San Augustine merchant who was Assistant Quartermaster General of the Texas Army in 1836. Sigler was born in North Carolina in 1790 and came to Texas by 1834.

[16] Dr. Archer was a native of Virginia who served in the state legislature before immigrating to Texas in 1831. He had been a delegate to the Convention of 1833 and was very active in the affairs of his new home.

[17] Wharton was born in Nashville, Tennessee in 1806 who came to Texas in 1833 after residing for a time in New Orleans. A lawyer by profession, he served for a brief time as a member of the General Council of the Provisional Government of Texas.

also a delegate from the District of Columbia, chairman of a committee to prepare a declaration of causes which impelled the colonists to take up arms against Mexico. Henry Millard[18], delegate from the District of Liberty, to draft a proposed provisional government for Texas.

On November 7, 1835, the Consultation adopted a "Declaration of Causes," in which they proclaimed their allegiance to the Federal Constitution of Mexico and declared that they were no longer bound by the social compact that created the United States of Mexico and that they were claiming their right to establish an independent government. The military despotism of General Santa Anna and his many unconstitutional actions were cited as causes for the break.

One week later, the plan for a Provisional Government was adopted. It called for the selection of a governor, lieutenant governor, and a legislative council composed of one member from each municipality represented in the consultation. The group also appointed Dr. Archer, Wharton, and Stephen F. Austin, commissioners to the United States, to obtain aid for the cause of Texas.

---

[18] Millard had been born in Mississippi in 1807. He immigrated to Texas in 1835 and at once became active in local affairs.

EARLY EAST TEXAS

Henry Smith[19], delegate from the District of Columbia, was chosen a Provisional Governor, and James W. Robinson[20], delegate from Nacogdoches, was named Lieutenant Governor. Sam Houston, delegate from the District of San Augustine, was elected commander in chief of the Texas Army, but this government was never successful in recruiting more than 100 troops for Houston's army.

Internal discord soon surfaced causing the provisional government to become helpless. Ultimately the council deposed Governor Smith and declared that Lieutenant Governor Robinson was Acting Governor of Texas. This temporary government was destroyed and displaced by the Convention of 1836.

Meanwhile, in September 1835 a small

---

[19] Smith was born in Kentucky in 1788 and came to Texas in 1827. He participated in the Battle of Velasco in 1832, was elected alcalde of Brazoria in 1833, and Political Chief of the Department of the Brazos in 1834.

[20] Robinson was born about 1800 in Hamilton County, Indiana. A lawyer by profession he immigrated to Texas in 1824. He would later take part in the Battle of San Jacinto in 1836.

EARLY EAST TEXAS

Mexican detachment of soldiers arrived at Gonzales with orders to commander a small 6-pound cannon that had been turned over to empresario Green DeWitt for use in defense against Indian attacks. Alcalde Andrew Ponton employed delaying tactics while dispatching runners to other settlements in the area calling for aid. A group of Texas volunteers equal in numbers to the Mexican forces soon arrived in Gonzales led by Colonel J. H. Moore. On October 2, 1835, the Texans crossed the Guadalupe River, attacked the Mexicans, and sent them in retreat toward San Antonio. The Texas Revolution had begun.

The following month Stephen F. Austin was called to take command of the gathering Texas army and they immediately began a march toward San Antonio. Captain George Collinsworth with a detachment of troops captured Goliad and a large supply of foods and ammunition. By October 24, the Texans had driven the Mexicans back to San Antonio and undertook a siege. In November Austin was replaced by Edward Burleson so that Austin could proceed with his commission to seek aid in the United States.

Thereafter in early December a force of some 300 volunteers, led by Ben Milam, began an assault on the old colonial capital. After five days of battle, the Mexican commander surrendered the town, but Ben Milam was killed during the assault. The

EARLY EAST TEXAS

Mexicans were permitted to return to Mexico after agreeing that they would not again oppose the reestablishment of the Mexican Constitution of 1824. The ease with which they had captured the town led the Texans to place a very low estimate on the fighting ability of the Mexicans and to conclude the revolution was over.

In pursuance of an order issued by the 1835 Consultation, elections were held on February 1, 1836 to select delegates to attend a convention to meet March 1 at Washington-on-the-Brazos. Robert Potter, John S. Roberts, Thomas J. Rusk, and Charles S. Taylor,[21] represented the Nacogdoches Municipality; Edwin O. Legrand and Martin Parmer,[22] the

---

[21] Potter was born in June 1799 in Granville, North Carolina. He joined the United States Navy as a midshipman and served four years. He later became a lawyer, served two terms in the North Carolina legislature and one term in the Congress of the United States. He was the first Secretary of the Navy of the Republic of Texas.

[22] Legrand, a native of North Carolina, had been born about 1795 came to Texas by 1835. He participated in the Battle of San Jacinto and the Siege of Bexar. He was also Chief Justice of San Augustine County.

EARLY EAST TEXAS

Municipality of San Augustine; William C. Crawford and Sydney O. Pennington[23], the Municipality of Shelby; and James T. Gaines, the Municipality of Sabine.

The assembled delegates first drafted and signed a declaration of independence;[24] Next, a committee composed of one delegate from each municipality was chosen to draft a constitution for the

---

[23] Crawford was a native of Fayetteville, North Carolina, having been born there in there in 1804. In 1830 he was licensed as a Methodist minister and was immediately assigned to a circuit in Georgia. Thereafter, he preached two years in Florida before coming to Texas in 1835 where he settled in the Tenaha Municipality near Shelbyville. Pennington was born in Christian County, Kentucky in 1809 but immigrated first to the Arkansas Territory before coming to Texas in 1834. He settled in the Tenaha Municipality. He participated in the Siege of Bexar collected supplies for the Texas Army during the Revolution.

[24] James Gaines was one of five committee members who drafted the declaration.

EARLY EAST TEXAS

Republic of Texas.[25] Thomas J. Rusk was appointed to the committee to edit the committee's draft, and records demonstrate that he was more responsible than any other delegate for its final wording. The final document created a government modeled closely upon those of the United States and some of the states of the American South. During the final hours of the convention erroneous rumors that the Mexican cavalry was only fifty miles away prompted a hasty adjournment.

While the convention delegates were being selected and the convention at work, developments in the field proved discouraging for Texan's hopes. In early March a force of some 150 men under the leadership of Frank W. Johnson and James Grant was destroyed almost to the last man by General Jose Urrea's Mexican calvary. Near the middle of the month, Colonel James W. Fannin and his command was defeated near Coleto Creek and subsequently massacred on orders of General Santa Anna. Also early in the month the Mexican general's army of some 6,000 men besieged the Alamo, took it by storm, and slew its defenders.

One of the final actions of the 1836

---

[25] Martin Parmer, Robert Potter, James Gaines, William C. Crawford were East Texas members of this committee.

EARLY EAST TEXAS

Convention was the appointment of one of the delegates, Sam Houston, commander in chief of the Texas Army. He immediately went to south Texas and assumed command. When he learned of the advance of a Mexican command larger than his own 600 men, he retreated toward the Brazos River arriving at San Felipe in late March.

When news of Houston's retreat was carried eastward into the settlements by fleeing civilians and soldiers who had left with and without official leave, widespread fear was created, and the frontier began folding back toward the east. Loading wagons, oxcarts, sleds, or horses, the frantic settlers, mostly women and children, began a desperate rush to keep ahead of the Mexican army. Their actions known as the "Runaway Scrape," effectively depopulated the western and central parts of the state.

The temporary government created by the 1836 Convention also fled as the Mexican forces advanced. Its headquarters was moved from Washington-on-the-Brazos to Harrisburg near present-day Houston and from there to Galveston Island.

Houston continued to retreat eastward until he ultimately reached a spot where Buffalo Bayou joins the San Jacinto River. On April 20, 1836, Santa Anna's advance party pitched camp with Houston's army deployed before him. The following day, the Texans launched a surprise attack on the Mexican

EARLY EAST TEXAS

force that resulted in an eighteen minute battle, the Battle of San Jacinto, in which 630 Mexican soldiers were killed and 730 captured, among them the Mexican general.

On May 14, 1836, President General Santa Anna signed a public and a secret treaty with the Republic of Texas. In the public treaty he proclaimed that all hostilities between the two nations would cease immediately and his Mexican troops would withdraw south of the Rio Grande. In the secret treaty he pledged to work to gain diplomatic recognition of Texas as a sovereign nation, to sign a trade agreement with the Republic of Texas, and to acknowledge the Rio Grande as the boundary between the two nations.

Revolutionary Days in East Texas

The Battle of Nacogdoches fought in August 1832 marked the beginning of a new era for Nacogdoches and all of East Texas. It ended the first phase of the struggle between the Mexicans and the Anglo colonists. From that point, the character of Nacogdoches became steadily more Anglo Texan and Anglos became more firmly entrenched elsewhere in the region. Thereafter, Nacogdoches and the Redlands, instead of posing a danger from Mexican troops in the rear of the colonists' struggles in the western portion of the colony became a reserve of strength and support and a possible refuge in time of disaster.

A brief period of relative quiet following the battle allowed the ayuntamientos of the settlements to turn their attention to local matters. At least two important steps taken by the Convention of 1832, however, directly affected the settlers in East Texas. The first of them was the creation of a central control committee of Vigilance, Safety, and Correspondence with sub-committees in all districts. These committees kept the President and General Council constantly informed on the state of affairs in the more distant districts throughout the time of revolution.

The second involved the adoption of a plan for the organization of a militia force in each district. The plan called for each district to furnish one regiment of militia for use in any military action when circumstances required. It also required all able-bodied men capable of bearing arms be organized into companies with the appropriate officers.

A meeting held in Nacogdoches in the summer of 1835 perhaps best illustrates the sentiment prevalent in East Texas on the eve of the Revolution. Its presiding officer, John Forbes, later wrote that the Redlanders would join with other Texans to maintain their liberty and rights and would stand shoulder to shoulder with them in defense of republican institutions and support of the laws of their adopted country. From the records of the meeting, it apparent that the idea of independence had not yet taken hold among the people of East Texas, remote as they were from the immediate threat of violence. They almost certainly were inclined to peace, if peace be possible.

As time passed that summer East Texans began regretfully and reluctantly to turn away from their loyalty to Mexico and Mexican institutions because they came to understand that their loyalty had been betrayed and ignored. What emerged was a determination to resist to the utmost the efforts of the Mexican government and its officials to reduce them to a state of political bondage. Even at this late stage in the progression toward revolution a large segment of the Mexican settlers in East Texas was in sympathy with them, and it was not until all parties had been embittered by events during the war that antagonistic feeling were engendered on both sides.

Late in the year immediate enrollment of volunteers capable of bearing arms was hampered by the scarcity of weapons and by the lingering doubt concerning the attitude of Indians in the area. When the Cherokee leaders rejected Mexican offers of an alliance and pledged to remain on their lands, preparations for war began everywhere in East Texas.

While all these developments were unfolding, Nacogdoches and all of East Texas remained a frontier area populated for the most part by the rough

EARLY EAST TEXAS

and ready people usually found in such places. Moreover, immigrants from the United States continued to pour through the Sabine gateways on their journeys to the interior. Many liked the towns or their surrounding countryside and decided to stay. Several hundred Indians: Choctaws, Seminoles, and others from the Creek Nation, also crossed the Sabine River and alarmed local officials. Other immigrants, deserters from the armies of the United States and Mexico, came in sufficient numbers to cause the Nacogdoches Ayuntamiento to pass resolutions regulating their conduct and manner of living.

Even as the clouds of impending war gathered, immigrants still poured across the Sabine River boundary. In Nacogdoches alone, from January to December 1835, 822 entrance certificates relative to admission to settle in Texas were issued by Nacogdoches officials. Even after war had been declared they continued coming.

During the winter of 1835 and the spring of 1836, volunteers for the Texan army continuously passed through Nacogdoches and other frontier settlements on their way to fight for independence. Groups of men from the United States numbering in the hundreds poured through Nacogdoches alone.

An old record book kept by a San Augustine recruiting officer shows that during May and June of 1836 five companies entered Texas military service in

EARLY EAST TEXAS

his jurisdiction. Of these men, fifty-four came from Georgia, 107 from Kentucky, and forty-five from Tennessee. Thus, for months after war's end American volunteers continued to cross the Sabine River in search of adventure and an opportunity to fight for the cause of liberty.

After news of the Texan victory at San Jacinto and the gradual return to order spread and as people learned of that it was a total victory, and that the government was again functioning, many of those who had taken part in the "Runaway Scrape" slowly began returning to their homes. By midsummer even the most hesitant had recrossed the Sabine River and headed for home. News stories reported that crops in East Texas were better than they had been in many years and that those who had not been able to plant crops until after the Battle of San Jacinto would be able to supply their needs.

In the aftermath of the war, county militia units continued to muster at least twice a year from 1837 through 1844. The East Texas militia companies formed the Third Brigade, Texas Militia, and they were called to actual service in the field at least three times during the period of the Republic in 1838, 1839, and 1844.

The smoke of battle had hardly disappeared at San Jacinto before the Texas farmers in Houston's army began quietly to drift away. They were simply

EARLY EAST TEXAS

going home to farm, family, and friends. They were superb fighting men, but they were not soldiers. They were unpaid troops who volunteered only for the current emergency and who had crops to gather. Within a few short weeks, virtually every Texas private soldier, both volunteer and regular army men, had departed for home.

Veterans of the Revolution were restive. They were unpaid, short on supplies, and demanding the land bounty of as much as 320 acres they had been promised when they enlisted. In the face of continued unrest among the military, in July, 1836, David G. Burnet, ad interim president of the Republic, called for a general election in September to create a new, permanent Texas government. Texans were to choose a President, Vice President, fourteen Senators, and twenty-nine Representatives; ratify the proposed constitution for the Republic; and indicate their desire to seek annexation as an American state.

Sam Houston was elected President, M. B. Lamar became Vice President; the Constitution was ratified unanimously; and the proposition to seek annexation carried by more than thirty to one. When these men took office, twenty-three counties formed the Republic of Texas and a modified American flag-- red, white, and blue emblazoned with a single five-pointed star--waved over the temporary capitol at Columbia.

EARLY EAST TEXAS

For the settlements on the eastern frontier a new period of development was launched as well. They began this new phase under the familiar laws and customs which they had inherited from their Anglo-American ancestors. They had experienced little or no oppression or violence under Mexican rule, and the personal freedoms of the people had not been unduly interfered with. Only Nacogdoches had been occupied by an armed garrison and had known violence and warfare.

The area suffered from the lack of government rather than any excess of one. Governments had long neglected to enforce the civil laws and had pursued a vacillating and devious policy toward the danger represented by the Indians situated to the north. The danger of Mexican attempts to reoccupy Texas also alarmed them.

Having suffered through a season of transitory and ineffective temporary government, East Texans welcomed the inauguration of a government sustained by a written constitution. Many of them realized that difficulties would be encountered and that their mettle would be tested, but they also sensed that there would never be a return to the events that preceded San Jacinto.

EARLY EAST TEXAS

CHAPTER SEVEN

EVENTS IN THE LIFE OF THE REPUBLIC

The Republic of Texas, as described by an eminent Texas historian, was a struggling frontier community of less than 40,000 people made up of a series of plantations and farms carved out of the Southern forests along the river bottoms extending north from the Gulf of Mexico. Most settlers were subsistence farmers who practiced a little bartering on the side. The largest towns were frontier outposts with mud streets with at most a few thousand inhabitants. There were no banks or improved roads or organized schools.

Over this sprawling community governments were only loosely organized. The old Spanish-Mexican ayuntamiento was rapidly replaced with the tractional southern county, but, in reality, the real government consisted primarily of sheriffs and justices of the peace. In East Texas, the municipalities of the old Department of Nacogdoches were designated as original counties of the Republic. In 1836, the municipalities of Liberty, Jefferson, Jasper, Sabine, San Augustine, and Shelby were created as counties with the same names. The remainder of the area east of the Trinity River was designated as the

EARLY EAST TEXAS

County of Nacogdoches. Later at least twenty counties were carved out of the original Nacogdoches County: Anderson, Angelina, Camp, Cherokee, Dallas, Delta, Gregg, Henderson, Hopkins, Houston, Hunt, Kaufman, Raines, Rockwall, Rusk, Smith, Trinity, Upshur, Van Zandt, and Wood.

The new nation was faced with a number of serious problems, among them were establishment of the framework of government, diplomatic recognition by the powers of the world, creation of a stable financial system, peace with the Indians, revival of the war with Mexico, promotion of annexation.

During the early days of the Republic, two European visitors visited Nacogdoches and recorded their impressions of a frontier outpost. A German immigrant related that the original Spanish settlers had built homes known as jacales. They were mud and log structures that now looked old and woebegone. The Anglo Americans, on the other hand, had built a number of elegant framed houses, well furnished and painted white. These homes were scattered along and among the ancient log and mud "hovels." He observed that prior to the Revolution many Mexicans had lived in the town, but since that time most of them had moved westward toward San Antonio. Those who remained were looked upon with distrust by the emerging majority of Anglo Texans who regarded them as thinly disguised enemies.

EARLY EAST TEXAS

A distinguished visitor from Virginia recorded similar impressions. He was struck by the fact that the Roman Catholic (or Mexican) burial ground was located among several mounds on the north side of the town while the cemetery for Protestants (or Anglo-Texans) was located several hundred yards from it on the east side of town.

He too described the buildings of the town with a few exceptions as miserable, shabby, old Mexican jacales constructed by inserting pickets in the ground, fastening them at the top with a plate, and daubing the interstices with red mud. Others were constructed on logs covered with clap-boards with chimneys of red mud. As for the residents themselves there were a number of Anglo American families intermixed with families with Spanish surnames, but much "ill blood" existed between them.

The Cordovan Rebellion

Along with other communities in East Texas, Nacogdoches experienced a period of relative calm in 1836 as the new national government and reorganized local governments began to function, but that tranquil state of affairs was not destined to endure for more than two years. Under the surface calm was fact that most citizens of Mexico did not recognize the independence of Texas, considered the defeat at San

EARLY EAST TEXAS

Jacinto as only a temporary loss, and formulated plans to reclaim the errant province. Moreover, many Mexican nationals living in Texas were dissatisfied with the outcome of the Revolution and resented having to become citizens of the new predominantly Anglo American nation.

As early as March 1837, vague rumors of an intended attack on the towns of Nacogdoches and San Augustine by a combined force of Mexicans in the vicinity and the Indians in Northeast Texas were circulating, but they were generally ignored as no outward sign of hostilities appeared. Subsequent reports convinced many that a widespread conspiracy was being created. In late August a Mexican man was killed on the Red River who was carrying instructions from Mexican General Vincente Filsola directed to Texas Mexicans and friendly Indians. Other documents in his possession indicated that the general was secretly visiting those East Texans for the purpose of inciting them to insurrection.

In East Texas the principal one of these unhappy Mexicans was Vicente Cordova. He had arrived in Nacogdoches as early as 1826 were he was active in community affairs. He participated in the Battle of Nacogdoches, served as the town's alcalde, a regidor, and as a primary judge. He was an outspoken opponent of the movement for Texas independence who, in 1836, attempted to recruit

EARLY EAST TEXAS

volunteers from the East Texas region to resist the effort to separate Texas from Mexico. Failing in that endeavor, in the summer of 1838, Cordova organized a group of dissatisfied Mexicans and their Indian allies to recapture Texas for the Mexican nation.

Cordova had become disenchanted with the Texas Revolution when the participants ceased to support the Mexican Constitution of 1824. In 1838, he and his allies dispatched a letter to President Sam Houston disavowing their allegiance to the Republic of Texas. This action weas followed by enlisting the aid of various Indian tribes, principally the Cherokees, who had long been unhappy about their treatment at the hands of the Texans.

He gathered his forces together at a camp near the Angelina River and planned an attack. Meanwhile the preacher and congregation of a small rural church in the same area came into Nacogdoches to notify authorities that a rebel force had gathered, and about the same time a party of the town's residents, searching for stolen horses, also discovered and reported the assembled force. John Durst and a company of scouts were dispatched by General Thomas J. Rusk to locate Cordova's encampment. The scouting party discovered the rebels camped across the Angelina River in present-day Cherokee County. According to Antonio Menchaca, who had visited the rebel camp, there were about 120 Mexicans and

EARLY EAST TEXAS

twenty-five Biloxi and Iones Indians present.

General Rusk issued a call for volunteers to suppress the uprising, and approximately 1,000 East Texas militiamen responded. The General then deployed his forces at strategic points in the area. Thereafter, on August 9, a company of volunteers from Douglass in Nacogdoches County reported that their scouts had been fired on at the lower crossing of the Angelina River. They were ordered to hold their position while Rusk gathered three companies, about 100 men, and rushed to their aid. On arrival at the river, Rusk learned that the report was false, but he soon learned that the rebels were gathered in force farther up the opposite bank of the river.

While awaiting reinforcements and scouting the river crossings, Rusk determined that Cordova had been joined by additional Indians. While he waited General Rusk was joined by a company of 120 militiamen from San Augustine under the command of Major Henry W. Augustine, a detachment from Shelby County under the command of Colonel Landrum, a number of other smaller groups, increasing the strength of his forces to some 600 men.

Determining that the rebels were moving toward a union with the Cherokees, Rusk detached Major Augustine and his San Augustine militiamen to pursue Cordova while he marched the remainder of his troops to the Cherokee village. Before he reached the Cherokee village, Rusk received word that many of the Mexicans had dispersed. Finding the Indians peaceful, he returned to Nacogdoches and discharged his troops.

After being pursued for a time, Cordova and a part of his band managed to reach Mexico in the spring of 1839. He returned to Texas with General Adrian Woll's invading force in 1842 and was slain at the Battle of Salado. Thirty-three of his rebels were eventually captured and held for trial in Nacogdoches. A grand jury then indicted thirteen of them for treason. A second grand jury indicated the remaining twenty for the same offense.

Four of their number: Antonio Menchaca, Estevan Mora, Jose Procella, and Jose Antonio Peres, alleging that they could not receive a fair trial in Nacogdoches were granted a change of venue to San Augustine. Ultimately thirty-two of the prisoners were transferred to San Augustine. On January 7, 1839, at a special term of the district court presided over by Judge Shelby Corzine, all were found innocent except Antonio Menchaca.

The Mexican was sentenced to be hanged, but President M. B. Lamar pardoned him on the ground that seven of the jurors at his trial reported that they had agreed on a verdict of guilty only after they had been confined in the San Augustine jury room for two days. Thus, the Cordovan Rebellion never posed a serious threat, but a more dangerous potential for trouble loomed.

The Cherokee War

During President Sam Houston's first administration, troops were kept out of the Indian county, and the president's Indian policy which favored friendship and peace combined to allow the new government to avoid serious wars with them. The most threatening situation was that of relations with the Cherokees some of whom had entered Texas as early as 1819 and occupied lands just to the north and west of the East Texas settlements. The Spanish government had given them vague promises of land grants in the vicinity; the Consultation of 1835 had promised them the lands they occupied, and in February 1836, Houston and John Forbes[26] acting on authority granted them by the Consultation negotiated

---

[26] Forbes, native of Ireland, was born in 1797 and immigrated to the United States in 1817, settling in Ohio with his parents. In 1834, he moved his family to Nacogdoches where be became chairman of the Committee of Vigilance and Public Safety the following year. He was commissary general of the Texas Army at the Battle of San Jacinto.

EARLY EAST TEXAS

a treaty with them providing for permanent title to their land. The Senate of the Republic of Texas failed, however, to ratify the treaty.

The rejection of their claims added to the slow but steady encroachment of their lands by white settlers created ever increasing friction between the settlers and the Cherokees, Kickapoos, and Shawnees. More animosity was generated in 1838 when General Thomas J. Rusk and his army of militiamen began to march on the Cherokees in an effort to intercept and capture Vicente Cordova, only to discover that the Mexican rebel had not sought shelter among them. Later that same year Rusk with a force of 230 soldiers pursued a band of Kickapoos, destroyed their village, and killed eleven of their warriors.

Thereafter, sporadic raids in 1838 and 1839 upon white settlers by Indians further escalated the growing friction between the two groups. In May 1839, East Texans learned that the Mexicans planned to enlist the aid of the Indians against the Texas settlers in keeping with their plan to recapture the errant province. M. B. Lamar, who had been inaugurated as the second president of Texas in late 1838, initiated a greatly changed Indian policy. Lamar, Secretary of War Albert S. Johnston, and Commissioner of Indian Affairs G. W. Bonnell agreed upon a policy of severity. In this they were supported by the Congress of the Republic.

EARLY EAST TEXAS

President Lamar's policy was grounded on a traditional Anglo American belief that Indians could not and did not own the land, they were merely tenants at will. Thus, white settlers might dispossess them without formal legal action. By this time the belief had acquired the legitimacy of two hundred years of practice. Time after time, events had demonstrated that governments could not prevent white settler encroachment on Indian lands, and that if the natives resisted, then governments failed to afford them protection and assistance.

As a part of that policy President Lamar determined to expel the Indians from East Texas. In July 1839, Kelsey H. Douglass[27] was put in command of about 500 militiamen under the overall command of Edward Burleson, Willis H. Landrum, and Thomas J. Rusk and ordered to move the Indians out of Texas into the western section of the Arkansas Territory, today's State of Oklahoma.

Douglass' army marched to Council Creek and camped six miles south of the principal Cherokee village of Chief Bowles. Army leaders met with Bowles and other prominent Cherokees and negotiated a treaty of removal which the Indians later

---

[27] Douglass had come to Texas in October 1835, settling in Nacogdoches where he established a mercantile business.

refused to sign objecting to a clause providing for an armed escort out of the Republic of Texas.

This action provoked an attack on the village on July 15 which came to be known as the Battle of the Neches. The site of this battle was a few miles west of Tyler in what is now Henderson County. Texan casualties numbered three killed and five wounded; Indians lost eighteen killed. When the Indians fled the scene, Douglass made camp. But the following day the Texans pursued the Indians and engaged them near the headwaters of the Neches at a site in today's Van Zandt County. In this engagement Chief Bowles was slain along with a number of his warriors. A final fight near Grand Saline in Van Zandt County saw an estimated 100 Indians killed or wounded.

As late as July 24 the Texans were still pursuing the Indians, destroying their fields and huts, and sending the Indians fleeing to Cherokee lands outside the boundaries of the Republic. The Shawnees, less numerous than the Cherokees, were removed without bloodshed, and the Alabama and Coushatta Indians were removed to lands in the Big Thicket of East Texas.

In the view of many settlers, the expulsion of the Cherokees and Shawnees had removed the menace of Indian attacks from the region and opened up the lands to their north to Anglo settlement. Immigrants

EARLY EAST TEXAS

in large numbers took advantage of this opportunity, and in a few years enough of them had settled that this area was organized into counties and prosperous towns sprang up all through it. These new counties acquired the names of prominent early East Texans: Harrison, Henderson, Rusk, Houston, and Anderson.

The Regulator-Moderator Feud

Despite the removal of the threat of Indian incursions, trouble of a different kind loomed in the area. By 1839 a feud had developed in Shelby County that would ultimately involve all of East Texas before it ended. Trouble had been brewing for some ten to twelve years before a crisis developed. Its roots were embedded in the easy access to Shelby County from the Neutral Ground to the east. During the years when little or no legal authority was exercised there, hundreds of desperadoes, outlaws, robbers, and other social outcasts took up residence and lived lives of almost completely unrestricted license, although in fear of each other.

After the Colonization Law of 1824 and later Texas independence, numbers of these desperate characters drifted across the Sabine River and settled along the border, most of them in Shelby but some in both San Augustine and Sabine Counties. There they continued to live their lawless lives.

EARLY EAST TEXAS

There were several types of these characters: Americans who had fled from justice seeking asylum, speculators dealing in fraudulent land titles, and members of an organized band of thieves, counterfeiters, robbers, and swindlers. Quietly, acting in the guise of honest voters, they elected cohorts to local offices and thereby gained immunity from the law.

Although in sheer numbers, this element did not constitute a majority or even a plurality of the citizens of Shelby County. The typical county resident was honest, honorable. and of high character. They had simply been duped into allowing this criminal element to gain control of local offices.

In 1839 a dispute between Joseph Goodbread and Sheriff Alfred George erupted that finally involved the whole county and spread to neighboring regions. George had sold a slave to Goodbread who received in payment a fraudulent land certificate. Later when the traveling Board of Land Commissioners[28] declared the certificate worthless,

---

[28] The traveling Board of Land commissioners was created by a statue of the Republic's Congress in 1840 to examine all county land records in counties east of the Brazos River and another to examine those west of the river. Each board was composed of three members.

EARLY EAST TEXAS

Goodbread demanded that George make good the price of the slave.

George contrived to involve Charles W. Jackson, ex-riverboat captain and fugitive from Louisiana, in the dispute. When Jackson encountered Goodbread on the streets of Shelbyville, he shot him to death. In July 1841 at Jackson's trial before District Judge John M. Hansford, a friend of Goodbread and the Moderators,[29] The Regulators disrupted the trial to the point that it could not proceed. The killer thus managed to escape punishment by the local court for the deed. He gathered together a band of men calling themselves the Regulators. Events soon demonstrated that the real purpose was to protect Jackson from acts of vengeance by Goodbread's friends.

One of the first actions of the Regulators was to attempt to arrest James Strickland and two McFadden brothers, well known friends of Goodbread. Failing to find them at home, they burned their houses and turned their families out in the winter cold. Foes of Jackson and the Regulators, then organized an opposing band known as the Moderators

---

[29] Jackson organized a band of men which he termed the Regulators, avowedly for the purpose of suppressing crime and other types of violence. Edward Merchant then organized a rival band to curb the activities of the Regulators.

EARLY EAST TEXAS

with Edward Merchant, John M. Bradley, and Deputy Sheriff James W. Cravens as their leaders.

Soon afterwards Jackson was ambushed and killed by Stricklands and McFaddens. At this stage Charles W. Moorman, a possible fugitive from Mississippi, replaced Jackson as the Regulator leader. Moorman then led a party bent on hunting down those implicated in Jackson's killing. They located most of the avengers twenty-five miles north of Crockett in Houston County, captured them, and returned them to Shelbyville for trial. At the trial they were found guilty, and all but one young man were hanged.

Moorman then enlisted a larger group of followers and took possession of the town of Shelbyville, and Moorman made his headquarters there. Moderators could visit the town only at risk of insult or injury. Under those conditions, matters were fairly quiet for a time until another killing caused violence to flare again.

A dispute between Regulator A. Henry Runnells, ex-Regulator Samuel N. Hall, and another Regulator named Stanfield. Ultimately Stanfield shot Hall in Shelbyville, was arrested, and placed in jail. Subsequently Stanfield escaped, inducing a group of Moderators to ambush him and Runnells. About this time John M. Bradley became the Moderator leader.

Following yet another trial, James Hall was killed, Bradley was ousted as Moderator leader, and

James M. Cravens assumed Moderator leadership. The Moderators then determined to occupy Shelbyville. The feuding groups then signed a truce in July 1844, but later that same month violence erupted once more.

About this same time Moorman made the tactical mistake of denouncing twenty-five of the leading citizens of Shelby County, placing them under the ban of exile or death. This action caused the better class of citizens in the county to join with Colonel Cravens, pledging themselves to restore law and order or die in the attempt. They soon had a band of some sixty-five men, and in the absence of the Regulators rode into Shelbyville and took over the town.

Both sides now recognized that a crisis was at hand and that one or the other must achieve a final victory or leave the county. Both sides began a vigorous recruiting campaign and soon had more than 100 men, and the entire population of the county felt constrained to join one side or the other. Moorman dispatched an appeal to the Regulator forces in nearby Harrison County causing two companies to come to his aid and raising his numbers to about 150 men. Cravens received additional recruits from Shelby and San Augustine Counties bringing his command to a total to some 165 men.

First one side and then the other gained ascendancy. On one occasion a band of seventy-five

Moderators marched through the town of San Augustine and camped in the woods along the Ayish Bayou. Thus, in 1844, Shelby County was in a deplorable condition. Men abandoned their homes and banded together for mutual safety. Farms were left untilled and growing up in weeds. Men were shot from ambush, prisoners were hanged, and other persons were driven from their homes.

Evidence points to the conclusion that nearly all of the men who ultimately engaged in this feud were small farmers who were recent immigrants to Texas. They had been persuaded to join one band or the other by unscrupulous men.

San Augustine County was treated to a sample of this lawlessness by the murder of John M. Bradley. The Regulators under Moorman's direction accused him of harboring their enemies and sought to have him killed, but he fortified himself in his own house and defied them. Attempting to avoid being slain, Bradley then left his home in Shelby County in 1844 and fled to San Augustine. Moorman learning of his whereabouts led a group of his Regulators down to the neighboring community. As Bradley was leaving a Baptist church service, Moorman shot and killed him.

Both sides then left Shelbyville and the Regulators erected fortified camps. The Moderators launched an attack at a camp at Hilliard's Spring and prepared to attack a second camp near Flat Fork

EARLY EAST TEXAS

Creek. As events seemed to be moving toward a bloody encounters, President Sam Houston paid a visit to San Augustine where he learned of the perilous situation in Shelby County.

Houston immediately issued a presidential proclamation calling on all citizens engaged in the feud to lay down their arms and retire to their homes. To reinforce his proclamation, Houston in August 1844 ordered Travis G. Broocks and Alexander Horton to take the militia forces of San Augustine, Sabine, Nacogdoches, and Rusk Counties and bring peace to East Texas.

With a force of some 600 men, Broocks and Horton arrested ten leaders from each side and brought them to San Augustine where a committee composed of District Judge William B. Ochiltree, Isaac Van Zandt, and Senator David S. Kaufman drafted an agreement disbanding both groups. They were instructed by Kaufman to disavow the names Regulators and Moderators and call themselves Texans, to forgive and forget, and resist any attempt to revive the feud.

By these means law and order was restored at last, and peace returned to Shelby County. When the Mexican War erupted in 1846 both Moderators and Regulators amicably joined together in Captain L. H. Mabbitt's Company, fraternized with each other, and were drawn into a common sympathy.

EARLY EAST TEXAS

Local Affairs

While Indian troubles, unrest among a portion of the Mexican citizenry, and a lingering feud occupied the attention of East Texans during the early years of the Republic of Texas, new system of local government were gradually being organized. By mid-year of 1837 the Spanish-Mexican scheme of alcalde, ayuntamiento, sindico, and the like was replaced by county judge, commissioners court, sheriff, clerk, justice of the peace, and constable of the traditional Southern county. Alcalde, regidores, and sindicos were succeeded by mayor, aldermen, secretary, and tax collector of American municipal governments.

Also in 1837 towns began to be incorporated by acts of the Congress of the Republic of Texas. Those statutes mandated that city officials be citizens of the Republic and owners of real estate within its corporate limits. Moreover, all residents of the incorporated town were required to keep hooks, ladders, and buckets available in case of fire.

In Nacogdoches, in the first city election leading residents were elected to office. Thomas J. Rusk became the first mayor, Henry Raguet, Charles H. Simms, John S. Roberts, Frost Thorn, Kelsey H. Douglass, James H. Starr, and Adolphus Sterne the first aldermen.[30]   Starr, who had arrived in Nacogdoches in 1838 recorded that he chose to settle there because the old town afforded an intelligent, cultured, and well-established society. An Ohio clergyman who visited the town in 1841 recalled that the old town contained about 300 to 400 people living together in a mixture of Spanish and American houses situated on a plain of white sand between two small creeks.

    The town of San Augustine was also incorporated in 1837 when James B. Johnson was elected mayor. During the same year Shelbyville was incorporated, but while the towns of Nacogdoches and San Augustine were growing, building buildings, tending to business, and working on nearby farms and

---

[30] Raguet was a leading town merchant, and planter, who had served as chairman of the Committee of Vigilance and Postmaster. Simms was also a town merchant and tavern keeper, Indian agent, and veteran of the Texas Revolution. Thorn yet another town merchant and the state's first millionaire. He served as a member of the legislature of the State of Coahuila y Texas and Chairman of the Committee of Vigilance. Starr was a physician and banker. He was President of the Nacogdoches Board of Land Commissioners and Secretary of the Treasury of the Republic of Texas.

EARLY EAST TEXAS

plantations, citizens of the Shelby County seat were embroiled in a conflict that stymied the growth of the town and blighted the community for years to come. In Sabine County, the town of Milam, the county seat, was likewise incorporated in 1837, but it too experienced slow growth during the time of the Republic. Local politics in these communities and elsewhere in the region were almost entirely personal. Men who were elected to office were popular favorites, often a hero of the Revolution, or those of marked ability.

The period from 1836 to 1860 constituted a distinct era in the life of the East Texas region. The men who were placed in charge of public affairs after independence who those who had entered Texas with the first high tide of immigration into the new nation. They and their descendants generally occupied the most important local and national offices.

Town life in most locales was full of vim and vigor. Business was transacted in a sedate and deliberate fashion. Men standing whittling on a board with their pocket knives may have just closed a deal involving thousands of acres of land. The man standing beside his loaded ox wagon may have just paid customs duties on a shipment of goods from the United States. Two others sitting on a log with a bundle of papers between them may be discussing the merits of thorny legal question. Mingled with these important transactions was a multitude of deals as mundane as shoeing a horse or the sale of a deer hide.

The responsibility for presiding over the course of county affairs looking to promotion of peace and prosperity was the chief justice of the county. That office was a survival from Mexican law and was soon replaced by that of county judge.[31] The Republic was also divided into a number of judicial districts presided over by district judges chosen by the Congress of the Republic. East Texas was placed in the First District and its judges given jurisdiction over civil suits involving more than $100 and criminal trials involving treason, murder, and other high crimes and misdemeanors.

During the life of the Republic of Texas county governments were the principal units of local government. Each county was governed by a county court composed of its chief justice who was elected by the Republic's Congress and two justices of the peace elected by qualified voters in their precincts. They were responsible for "superintendence and control of the public roads, bridges, and ferries and for the care

---

[31] Appendix I provides a list and other information concerning the district judges and chief justices of selected East Texas counties during the time of the Republic of Texas.

of the indigent, lame, blind, and poor persons who were unable to support themselves." In 1845 this arrangement was altered to replace the three-member county court by a commissioners court composed of the chief justice and four commissioners, all elected by voters in the county.

Other county officers required by the Constitution of the Republic were a sheriff, a coroner, and a convenient number of constables elected by the county voters. In addition, county voters were expected to participate in elections where members of the national Congress were selected. This bicameral legislature was composed of a House of Representatives that could not exceed forty members elected annually from their districts and a Senate that could never be less than one-third nor more than one-half of the number of the lower house. Senators served three year terms with one-third of the membership to be elected annually. In fact, the first House of Representatives was composed of thirty-four members, of which eight represented the four East Texas counties; the Senate numbered seventeen members, of which four were East Texans.[32]

One of the insoluble problems faced by

---

[32] Appendix II provides a list of the Congressmen from East Texas and other data concerning them.

EARLY EAST TEXAS

Spanish colonial officials and later by those of the Mexican governments was the control of smuggling that involved goods entering Texas from across the Sabine River. Separation from Mexico and creation of the Republic of Texas did not bring an end to the problem. The fiercely individualistic people of the region had long opposed any and all tariff levies. The only customs house created by the Congress of the Republic was located at San Augustine, although a clerk was also stationed in Nacogdoches. As a result smuggled goods were imported elsewhere without payment of customs duties, but merchants in San Augustine and Nacogdoches were forced to pay the tariffs. Merchants and other residents of the two towns pleaded for repeal throughout the life of the Republic but to no avail.

Smuggling goods across the Sabine River into and through Nacogdoches and other places in East Texas was a commonplace practice long before Gil Y'Barbo and his followers in 1779 reestablished the Nacogdoches settlement. Indeed, illicit trade was such a well established practice that smugglers had their own thoroughfares through all of East Texas. The rigidity of Spanish and Mexican regulations dealing with importing goods into the region coupled with the laxness of their enforcement and the closeness of French goods just across the Sabine River invited smugglers and smuggling. The settlers simply wanted, even needed, such products as cloth, cooking and eating utensils, salt, gunpowder, tools, coffee, and whiskey.

As a consequence, in time a Smugglers' Road or El Camino del Caballo (Horse or Mule Road) or Contraband Trace became a feature of economic life in East Texas. As early as 1780 this pathway from Natchitoches in western Louisiana to San Antonio and beyond was a well-known and well-established alternative to the King's Highway. From earliest colonial days to the eve of annexation it was used by traders, illegal immigrants, and others who wished to avoid customs duties and official inspection.

This trace was an Indian trail long before the Europeans came, and soon thereafter became the first cattle trail in Texas. In the days of the Republic, therefore, it was a well-beaten track. By that time through Nacogdoches County there were two routes of El Camino Real, the Upper and Lower Roads, with the El Camino del Caballo near them. Users almost invariably went one way and returned the other to avoid easy detection.

The King's Highway and the Smugglers' Trace were not the only routes through East Texas. Hundreds of Indian and animal trails criss-crossed the forest. One well-marked route went through Crockett in Houston County west to the Trinity River landing. Others led to nearby Indian villages and to settlements of the French and Spanish along the rivers. Many of them also led to or crossed the Upper and Lower San Antonio Road.

Smugglers' Trace follows the Angelina River about half its distance through Nacogdoches County. It leaves the river there and proceeds straight to the Attoyac River, then proceeds well south of Nacogdoches to the Spanish Bluff Crossing of the Angelina, and from there southwest out of the region. Throughout all those years, smuggling and Smugglers' Trace played an important role in the economic life of East Texans.

EARLY EAST TEXAS

CHAPTER EIGHT

EDUCATION AND RELIGION

With the Revolution over and East Texas beginning to settle down in the ways of peace, the citizens of the East Texas communities began to give serious consideration to providing at least elementary schools for their children. Teachers usually received cordial receptions, but East Texas parents found it difficult to find means of conducting schools. In keeping with the Southern tradition in America they continued to follow the English system for educating the youth. This meant that they relied on private schools and institutions of higher learning.

They discovered, however, that relying on private schools for instruction was fraught with problems where money and books were at a premium. Protestant ministers took the lead in educating the youth of their communities. Texas preachers--particularly Methodists, "Old School" Presbyterians, and Protestant Episcopalians--taught a variety of schools and actively promoted the establishment of elementary schools, academies, and "colleges." And after the annexation of Texas to the United States a statewide convention dominated by those preachers took the first steps toward standardization of teacher

EARLY EAST TEXAS

training and instructional methods.

Education in East Texas

An 1830 statute enacted by the legislature of the State of Coahuila y Texas provided for the creation of elementary schools, but the ayuntamientos of both Nacogdoches and San Augustine reported that it was impossible for them to provide capable teacher for the government-mandated schools. Instructors who were fluent in both Spanish and English were almost certainly not obtainable. In addition, poverty stricken colonists were in no mood to tolerate any attempt by Mexican authorities to introduce a system of tax-supported schools.

After the Revolution, the Congress of the Republic granted four leagues (17,712 acres) of public land to each county for the creation of public schools, and designated the chief justice and two associate justices of the county as a school board to administer the schools. Despite this generous endowment a system of public common schools was never established in the Republic. A public school was established in only one town, Houston.

In the decade of the life of the Republic Houston attracted more teachers than any other town. In addition to schools for girls, young ladies, and small boys taught by women, private schools taught

EARLY EAST TEXAS

by male teachers were available for older male youths.

Where ordinary rural or village schools existed they were in session from early morning until nearly sundown. Textbooks, in all subjects, were always at a premium. Virtually all schools from elementary to those offering college-level courses closed their sessions with public examinations. Education of children in strictly rural districts was even more difficult than in the towns. In those nearly isolated areas, mothers attempt to provide a modicum of education or families would combine their resources to employ teachers. Many of those rural school teachers were ill trained and regarded teaching as only a temporary means of subsistence. The time and length of the terms were regulated by the state of the weather, the condition of crops, and the likelihood of Indian attacks.

In the early years of the Republic, the two East Texas town of San Augustine and Nacogdoches demonstrated comparatively high cultural levels among their citizens and considerable intellectual attainments. The citizens of San Augustine almost immediately following the return of peace began to consider seriously ways and means of providing an adequate system of education for their children.

Their first move was the establishment of San Augustine University. The act of Congress incorporating the university was passed in 1837 on the same day on which the town itself was incorporated. The newly created university was also granted four leagues of public land as an endowment. A Board of Trustees created to oversee the school was composed of residents of the town and of the surrounding country, at least half of them living from five to ten miles from the county seat. It contained members of all the religious denominations then represented in the county and of a variety of public opinions.[33]

The trustees were not able to get much accomplished, however, until 1840 when they traded one league of the endowment for a large building erected in the eastern section of the town. It was a frame structure of about forty or fifty feet square with a basement, three stories, and a cupola or observatory in the center. Two more years passed before the trustees were able to secure a qualified person to fill the position of principal.

The man they selected was the Reverend

---

[33] The Board was composed of Elisha Roberts, Jesse Burditt, William McFarland, John Cartwright, Sumner Bacon, George Teal, Augustus Hotchkiss, Henry W. Augustine, Andrew J. Cunningham, Philip A. Sublett, Iredell D. Thomas, Albert G. Kellog, Almanzon Huston, William W. Holman, and Dr. Joseph Rowe.

EARLY EAST TEXAS

Marcus A. Montrose, a Scotsman, a graduate of the University of Edinburgh, and a Presbyterian minister. He had immigrated to the United States about 1839 at age thirty-one. He served as President of the University in 1845 when he resigned to take charge of a new university just established in Nacogdoches.

Soon after the university was established its trustees formed an alliance with the Presbyterian Church, and the church agreed to support the institution. In 1843, the local Presbyterian congregation subscribed about 4,500 acres of land to help provide that support. In this fashion, the university became in effect a Presbyterian school. The method of teaching employed laid stress on developing the mental powers of the upper class students by using them partly as teachers in the lower classes in a system of monitors and assistants.

San Augustine University encountered severe difficulties. Lack of proper textbooks, stress generated by financial pressures, selection and retention of qualified teachers, and creation of sectarian jealousy proved serious handicaps. Although the institution was nominally a public institution, it was, in fact, a Presbyterian school. The town itself was a strong Methodist center with three resident ministers having homes there. As the result of their strenuous effort they were able to establish Wesleyan College with the sanction and support of the Methodist Church. Rivalry between the two institutions was inevitable and became intense.

As a result by 1845 the prosperity of San Augustine University was beginning to wane. Attendance which at one time reached 150 students was reduced to about fifty. President Montrose resigned and was replaced by the Reverend James Russell, a teacher in the school. Russell, another Scotsman and graduate of the University of Edinburgh, was a concise writer and an accomplished lecturer; but he proved to be a man of irascible, impetuous temperament, and dominating personality.

In 1847, President Russell published an article in the Redlander, the town's newspaper, defaming a female resident of the town. Whereupon, on August 10 her brother, Henry Kendall, shot and killed the Presbyterian minister. With his death the activities of the university came to an end. It had long been losing patronage, and Russell's death brought about its demise.

The controversial sermons of President Montrose prompted the substantial number of Methodists among the town's residents to embark on the creation of a university founded and maintained by the Methodist Church. Reverend Francis Wilson devoted himself to the establishment of the college and traveled far and wide promoting interest in the proposed institution. He was ably seconded by the

Reverend Littleton Fowler and the endorsement of the Annual Conference.

A fund of some $20,000 was accumulated and used to erect and furnish a three-storied building. The structure was about forty by eighty feet, well lighted, and situated on a spacious campus. A charter for Wesleyan College was enacted by the Congress of the Republic in 1844 and appointed fourteen trustees, among them Francis Wilson, Littleton Fowler, and Daniel Poe, all Methodist ministers, and included James Pinckney Henderson, who would soon become the first Governor of the State of Texas.[34]

For a few years the college functioned efficiently but uneventfully, but in 1846 the fortunes of the institution began to decline. Debts piled up and income was never sufficient to meet expenses and retire the debt. The end came in 1847 when Bishop Capers announced its demise. The two educational institutions came to an end about the same time for the same reasons. After the settlement of the Indian troubles and the opening of the vast interior of the region for settlement, numbers of the town's citizens

---

[34] Other trustees were John C. Brooke, Travis G. Broocks, James Perkins, Alexander M. Davis, F. G. Lovell, O. Fitzallen, Henry W. Augustine, John G. Berry, William D. Ratcliff, and John G. Love.

moved away to more promising fields. San Augustine ceased to be a port of entry. Both institutions lacked sufficient endowment and were almost entirely dependent upon local patronage for support. As the town lost population, that patronage failed and the colleges crashed.

Next residents of the town began to cast about for some means of replacing the defunct institutions. First, they tried to combine them into one school capable of maintaining itself. Toward that end the Congress passed an act in 1848 incorporating a new institution to be known as the University of East Texas. Its Board of Trustees was composed of fifteen representative citizens of San Augustine of all religious denominations represented in the county. No more than three trustees of any one denomination could serve at any one time. The property and endowment of the defunct University of San Augustine were transferred to the new university.

At the same time, the trustees of Wesleyan College combined with the trustees of the new institution and severed relations with the Methodist Annual Conference, thus uniting the two schools into one under the patronage of the Republic. No real effort was made, however, to carry this scheme into effect, and by 1850 it died a natural death.

Then, a new element entered the picture. In

EARLY EAST TEXAS

1850, the Redland Lodge No. 3 of the Masonic Order and the Rising Star Chapter No. 9 of the Eastern Star Order determined to unite to provide an adequate education for the youth of the community. From the beginning the new school was placed on a sound financial base. This new school did not aspire to becoming a university or even a modest college, but, instead, its sponsors gave it the more modest title of the Masonic Institute.

Free from the dissensions that had wrecked its predecessors, the Institute drew support from the whole county, its pupils being drawn from every station. Its Instruction was more fitting to the surroundings of a new country. It succeeded in providing a collegiate level of education until the ruin and desolation of the Civil War put an end to all projects of education beyond those of a simple common school.

During this same time the more affluent residents of Nacogdoches became interested in providing an education for their children, particularly their sons. They were rewarded in 1845 when in one of its last acts the Congress of the Republic chartered Nacogdoches University. A twenty-year charter required the school to be "equally open to the education of the children of persons of all classes, without regard to their religious belief."

The act transferred the four leagues (117,712

acres) of land granted to the ayuntamiento of Nacogdoches for purposes of education to the Nacogdoches University. All lands, buildings, and other public property of the institution were exempt from taxation for five years, and provisions were included for adding training in medicine and law when justified. In addition, the charter mandated that "no religious, sectarian, or other doctrines" were to be taught, Gilbert M. L. Smith was appointed the school's first principal, and his wife, Mary Smith, was named the drawing and printing teacher. The first school term the new institution enrolled 103 students, sixty males and forty-three females.

The University was governed by a fifteen-member Board of Trustees.[35] Private subscriptions of cash, land, lumber, pork, and labor supplemented the four-league grant. Private land donations by residents of the area such as James Harper Starr ($228.35 and 640 acres of land) brought the total land held by the trustees to 30,000 acres.

The first session of the new school was held in the old Red House, a frame and adobe building located just southwest of the Plaza Principal. Classrooms, an apartment for the principal and his

---

[35] Among the first trustees were Bennett Blake, Charles S. Taylor, Thomas J. Rusk, James Harper Starr, and Frost Thorn.

family, and a dormitory for male students occupied the lower floor and the upper story houses female students. The university occupied this building for the first seven years of its existence and spent the next three years in a building just across the street. In 1855, it moved about three blocks north to a building where classes were held for four years. Finally, in 1859, the university occupied its permanent home, a Grecian-style red brick structure on Washington Square. The Civil War was to jeopardize this educational effort as well as those in nearby San Augustine.

Efforts to provide education for younger children demonstrated a different story. Education in Spanish colonial Texas was designed to Christianize and domesticate the natives and to provide the rudiments of learning for the children of garrison troops and Spanish colonists. A mission school for the instruction of Indians was established as early as 1690 at San Francisco de los Tejas in East Texas. These mission schools taught Christianity, the Spanish language, and practical arts, but they achieved few permanent results. The difficulty of obtaining supplies, widespread illness among the pupils, and the indifference or hostility of the Indians combined to defeat their efforts.

A non-mission school was operating at San Antonio de Bexar as early as the 1740s, but it and other such schools established during this early period proved transitory. Efforts by colonial lawmaking bodies to compel parents to send their children to school were initiated in 1802, but the effort failed primarily because of the lack of funds. A decade later a public school was established at San Antonio that was supported by public funds, but it too did not last. The dominance of the military, frontier conditions, sparseness of population, poverty of the populace, and failure of the government to provide financial aid combined to ensure failure of all attempts to provide general education in the Spanish colonial period.

The Mexican Constitution of 1824 delegated the responsibility for education to the Mexican states. Thereafter, the Constitution of the State of Coahuila y Texas provided for the creation of elementary schools and seminaries in the principal towns of the state but did not provide any means of support. In 1829 the state government provided a plan for fee instruction of pupils whose parents were unable to pay tuition, but none was ever established.

In 1830, six primary schools for all of Texas were projected, at least one actually opened in Nacogdoches. But overall, plans for education in Mexican Texas were never implemented. For a variety of reasons then no system of public education ever developed in colonial Texas. A Spanish colonial official visiting Texas in 1834 observed that the San Antonio public school had been discontinued. He reported that the Department of Nacogdoches contained four municipalities and four towns, a population of 3,500 and there were three common schools in the department One was located in Nacogdoches, very badly supported, another in San Augustine, and the third in Jonesborough. He commented that the poverty of the people was extreme, that the state treasury lacked money, and that there was frequently friction in Nacogdoches between the Anglo Americans and the Mexicans.

During the colonial period, however, several private schools existed, some of which were subsidized by public funds. Instruction was provided in religion, morals, and the Three Rs. Ever plagued by lack of adequate funds, supplies, and competent teachers these private schools typically closed after a short time.

In the Anglo American settlements, the more affluent settlers sent their children to the United States for their education. As early as 1823, a few widely scattered "old field schools" and academies, similar to those in the American south sprang up. In those settlements parents who could not send their children away to private schools in the United States worried much about their childrens' future. Often, as soon as a dozen or more families had settled in any region or newly created town or county, they tried to organize a school. A building was erected or made available and a schoolmaster imported. Every family shared the cost of the teacher's salary which was often paid in land or commodities.

    Schools in Shelby County in this period provide examples of the typical rural system of East Texas. The first schools were almost certainly the Writing Schools common to all of early Texas. Writing teachers traveled from community to community during the summer months, between planting and harvesting times, holding two-week schools in local churches or abandoned cabins. In these schools children learned to write their ABCs and numbers, copied words, rhymes, and sentences from spelling books. After spending two weeks in several summers at such exercises, most children had obtained the basics of reading and writing. In addition Singing Schools taught those who attended tunes and words to a number of songs.

    The Constitution of the Republic of Texas directed its Congress to provide a system of public education. Although a few private schools were chartered during President Houston's first administration, more pressing problems demanded the attention of the new nation and prevented it from implementing a school system. In 1838, however, soon after his election as the Republic's second president M. B. Lamar urged the Congress to endow a system of public education.

EARLY EAST TEXAS

Thereafter, in 1839 and 1840, Congress adopted a plan for a school system ranging from the primary to the University level, delegated control over this to the county governments, and granted 17,712 acres of public lands to each county for the support of schools. Nevertheless, this plan failed to achieve its announced goals quickly because land prices were too low for sales to provide adequate revenue. In addition, there was an element of popular indifference on the county level to the establishment of schools. In fact as late as 1855 thirty-eight counties had made no effort to obtain their school land.

Private schools and academies of the type prevalent before the Revolution continued to operate, and several institutions of higher education were chartered. In spite of all efforts, prior to 1851 there were not really any but a few scattered schools in existence because of the Mexican War (1846-1848), the scant and scattered populace (212,592 in 1850), and scarce money (public debt estimated at $12.5 million).

Despite a number of near insurmountable obstacles, Texas made important strides toward the development of schools between the Battle of San Jacinto and Annexation. In 1836 there was a mere handful of teachers among an increasing population of Anglo Americans estimated at more than 25,000; in the succeeding ten years, the proportion of teachers rose dramatically. That development was achieved in spite of the persistent threat of Mexican and Indian attacks, violence rampant, and business growth disrupted by a disheartening depression.

Many of the newly arrived settlers were not financially able to support their children at school and needed their services at home. Others either did not appreciate the value of an education or believed that instruction by itinerant teachers was sufficient. Jealousies between neighboring towns hampered the development of unified support of colleges. In view of such difficulties, the progress made was indeed remarkable.

East Texas Religion

Nacogdoches, San Augustine, and Sabine-- these three communities were the cradles of both Roman Catholicism and Protestantism in Texas. The first Catholic mission sent from Mexico in Texas were located in East Texas primarily in order to have Spanish religious and military outposts on the extreme eastern boundary where they might counteract the activities of the French at Natchitoches in western Louisiana. The only ones that survived for any length of time were the Missions of Guadalupe at Nacogdoches and Dolores at San Augustine. The Spanish mission period came to an end in the early

EARLY EAST TEXAS

1770s leaving no lasting mark on the history of the region.

The return of Gil Y'Barbo and his colonists in 1779 marks the beginning of the parochial history of the Roman Catholic Church in East Texas. A church according to tradition was located on Church Square on the site of the present day County Courthouse and its priests ministered to the families of the parish that scattered to their various locations along the King's Highway. So far as San Augustine and much of the rest of East Texas was concerned ministrations by Catholic priests and continuation of Catholic Churches apparently came to an end with the coming of the filibustering expeditions of the early 1800s.

There is no existing account of the presence of a Catholic priest in the San Augustine district after the coming of the first Anglo American settlers in 1818 and especially after 1824 when the tide of immigration began to swell. Efforts of Catholic officials in Mexico to continue the work begun by Franciscan missionaries were hampered by revolutionary movements in Mexico itself, by long vacancies in ecclesiastical offices in northern Mexico, and by the lack of a sufficient number of parochial priests to minister to Catholics scattered over so vast an area. Thus, for several years prior to 1836 effective supervision of the Catholic church in Texas had ceased to exist, although a few dedicated priests ministered to their parishioners at San Antonio and Goliad and in the Irish colonies at Refugio and San Patricio.

Both Spanish and later Mexican colonization laws required all settlers to be at least nominally members of the Roman Catholic Church, and all Protestant services were strictly forbidden. Throughout most of Eastern Texas during the colonial period few of the Anglo American settlers were Catholics by faith and most were at best only nominal Roman Catholics. Indeed, most of them had little interest in formal religion of any kind. One observer wrote that conditions with respect to the gospel were superlatively bad, and yet another observed that there was little regard for the Sabbath which in general was observed in visiting, driving stock, and breaking mustangs.

The Anglo Americans had little cause to complain of spiritual persecution but on the contrary more cause to complain of spiritual neglect. In the San Augustine district, for example, there was no church or established place of worship. The reality that most of the inhabitants were really Protestants precluded any activity on their part on behalf of established religion and discouraged any missionary zeal on the part of priests in Nacogdoches. After the Cordovan Rebellion in 1838, virtually all the Mexican Catholic population of the district disappeared. Despite some inroads made by Protestant denominations during the period of independence and early statehood, Nacogdoches, on the other hand, remained predominantly Roman Catholic in religion.

Organized religion in the area now known as Shelby County did not play a major role in daily life. The thieves, cut throats, forgers, and fugitives who poured into the region were not receptive to attempts to "evangelize" them, and ministers were not held in high regard. Anglo settlers there as elsewhere almost universally ignored the legal requirement that all immigrants adhere to Roman Catholicism. Many were inheritors of a tradition of militant anti-Catholicism brought over from Europe by their ancestors. Moreover, the nearest Catholic mission was at San Augustine, a distance that discouraged travel.

Some colonial Texans did resent being deprived of the religious freedom they had enjoyed "back in the States," but most of them had little trouble reconciling themselves to the situation. The legal devise of marriage by bond removed one of the most urgent needs for clergymen. Some of the Anglo American settlers positively approved of the nonsectarian atmosphere they encountered in Texas.

In spite of official opposition and the indifference of many colonists, Protestantism made considerable inroads in colonial Texas. In the Ayish Bayou District during the period from 1818 to 1834,

EARLY EAST TEXAS

for example, many of the immigrants were members of Protestant churches in the states from which they came, and almost all of them were raised under the influences of Protestant surroundings. During that same period, however, adventurous Protestant missionaries began to cross the Sabine and preach. Since San Augustine was often the first town through which they would pass, the frequently expended their first missionary efforts in the town and in a radius of a few miles around the town. This area experienced the earliest beginnings of the Methodist, the Presbyterian, the Cumberland Presbyterian, and the Baptist churches in East Texas, and San Augustine became therefore a cradle of Protestantism in the Mexican province.

Among Protestant churches the Methodist was the first to enter this new field. As early as 1817, William Stevenson[36] preached at what was then called

---

[36] William Stevenson was born in South Carolina in 1768. His parents were members of the Presbyterian Church into which the son was baptized in infancy. In 1792 at age twenty-four he immigrated to Tennessee where eight years later he became a Methodist and soon thereafter was ordained a minister. In 1815 he affiliated with the Annual Conference of Tennessee and was sent to Mississippi. In 1816 he was placed on

EARLY EAST TEXAS

Jonesborough (Pecan Point) in present-day Red River County in northeast Texas. On his preaching tour in Texas, he also preached a sermon in Nacogdoches under the shade of what was known thereafter as "The Protestant Elm." In these early years of the century, Methodism was vigorously attempting to sending missionaries throughout the country. The Mississippi Annual Conference first began sending missionaries into Louisiana, and then looked eagerly at East Texas which was rapidly filling up with Anglo Americans.

Henry Stephenson[37], a Methodist minister located in Rapides Parish, Louisiana, also paid brief visits to Texas in 1824 and 1829 and held meetings along the Sabine River at which a good many Texans were converted and joined the Methodist Church. After the Mexican garrison was expelled from

---

circuit in the Arkansas Territory where four years later he was elected to the first Arkansas Territorial legislature.

[37] Henry Stephenson was born in Virginia in 1772 of Presbyterian parentage. In 1792 at age twenty he immigrated with his family to Kentucky and later to Missouri near St. Charles. By 1812 he had joined the Methodist Church and was licensed to preach. Along with his friend William Stevenson in 1826 he moved into northwestern Louisiana.

EARLY EAST TEXAS

Nacogdoches in 1832, Methodist missionaries became bolder and began proclaiming their doctrines openly across East Texas. That year Needham J. Alford[38], Methodist preacher, and Sumner Bacon[39], a Cumberland Presbyterian minister, held a two-day meeting near Milam in today's Sabine County in the face of vigorous opposition from Mexican authorities. At the same time Alford also preached in San Augustine.

The following year James P. Stevenson[40] held

---

[38] Alford at this time lived in Louisiana about twelve miles from the Sabine River.

[39] Bacon was born at Auburn, Massachusetts in 1790. After service in the U. S. Army and with a government surveying party Arkansas, in 1826 he was licensed to preach by the Cumberland Presbytery of Tennessee to come to Texas. He arrived in San Augustine in 1829 he preached throughout East Texas and as far into the interior as San Antonio.

[40] James Stevenson was born in Smith County, Tennessee in 1808, the son of William Stevenson. He joined the Methodist Church under his father's preaching in Louisiana. In 1831 he was licensed to preach by the Annual Conference of

three meetings in Sabine County, then a part of the San Augustine municipality. A two-day meeting was held near Milam, and two camp meetings were held at Samuel B. McMahan's[41] place, nine miles east of San Augustine. At the second of these meetings at regular church organization was established with forty-eight members and McMahan installed as Class Leader. This was the first Methodist Church organized within the known limits of the Republic of Texas. Meetings and other activities were held at Jonesborough in 1817 under the impression that the area was a part of the United States.

    Both Samuel and his son James B. McMahan became ordained ministers of the Methodist Church and were instrumental in spreading the Methodist Church throughout East Texas. They were also responsible for the organization of new Methodist churches in the area.

Mississippi and located in East Texas four years' later. He was a veteran of the Texas Revolution.

    [41] Samuel McMahan had come to Texas from Tennessee in 1831 locating about twelve miles east of San Augustine. He was converted to Methodism the next year and became one of the most influential Methodist leaders in East Texas.

EARLY EAST TEXAS

In June, 1834, Henry Stephenson on a preaching tour of San Augustine County organized a church at the home of George Teal, but it its members later scattered and the church dissolved. That same year Stephenson was appointed by the Mississippi Annual Conference to head a mission to Texas, whereupon he removed to Texas the next year and settled on Cow Creek, a branch of the Sabine River.

Almost all the activities of these early labors of Methodist ministers were within the boundaries of the newly organized Municipality of San Augustine which extended from the Sabine River on the east to the Attoyac River on the west. Their labors had resulted in the formation of two churches, one of which known today as McMahan's Chapel is still honored as the birthplace of Texas Methodism.

In 1837, soon after the Texas Revolution, American Methodist Bishops and the Board of Missions appointed three official representatives of the church to carry on the missionary work in Texas: Dr. Martin Ruter, Superintendent, Littleton Fowler and Robert Alexander, assistants. Alexander[42]

---

[42] Alexander was born in Smith County, Tennessee in 1811 and entered Texas in 1837 at age twenty six years. He united with the Methodist Church in 1828, and the following year was licensed to preach by the Annual Conference of Tennessee. He later

EARLY EAST TEXAS

hastened to Texas and preached his first sermon there in August 1837 before moving on to the McMahan settlement where he held a quarterly conference and organized the San Augustine circuit.

The same year Fowler[43] entered Texas by way of the Red River coming south to Nacogdoches and then on to Washington to meet Alexander. Ruter arrived in Texas in November 1837 where he preached a sermon at San Augustine before going on to Washington. During the coming year, three Methodist churches were erected: the first at San

---

transferred to the Alabama and then the Mississippi Conference. He then served the station at Natchez, Mississippi before coming to Texas.

[43] Fowler was born in Smith County, Tennessee in 1803 and moved in 1806 with his family to Caldwell County, Kentucky. In June 1820 he joined the Methodist Episcopal Church and was licensed to preach by the Annual Conference of Kentucky in 1826 and was appointed to the Red River circuit. He was sent to the Bowling Green station in 1828 and to the Louisville Station the following year. In 1832, he transferred to the Tennessee Conference and was stationed at Tuscumbia, Alabama. Until his removal to Texas in 1837, he was financial agent for LaGrange College in Tuscumbia.

Augustine, the second at McMahan's camp ground (McMahan's Chapel), and the third at Washington.[44] The church at San Augustine was the first Protestant Church to be built by any Protestant body west of their Sabine River.

By 1837, then, Protestant missionaries from the United States had begun entering Texas prepared to labor in the field. The custom was for one these ministers to stop at some settler's house and ascertain the family's religious inclination, and if he received a sympathetic response a time for services would be agreed on. The neighbors would be notified and religious services then held. If a small group responded, a church might be organized. When as many as three or four churches in the same area were formed, a larger organization would be organized. The Methodists would form a conference, the Presbyterians a presbytery, and the Baptists an association.

Slaves attended the services and became

---

[44] In 1837, Fowler obtained a deed for a church lot at Nacogdoches and with it $2,500 in subscriptions to build a church house. At the Annual Conference of 1854, the Nacogdoches Church reported a membership of 470 white individuals and 85 black persons who had been ministered to by five local preachers.

members of the church along with their owners. When there was a sufficient number of slaves, separate services were held for them. Nonsectarian Sunday Schools were established at many locations prior to a church being organized.

During this period great camp meetings were held over all of East Texas, and there were camp grounds in almost every community. People would come to these meetings from miles in every direction, sleeping in tents or in booths made of tree branches. In the center of the camp ground, oftentimes covered by an arbor made of brush laid on poles, was a rude pulpit, with seats made of logs, slabs, undressed planks, ranged in front of it. These meetings lasted for several days and nights with preaching three times each day. They featured impassioned sermons, fervent prayers, calling for mourners, shouting, conversions, and ecstatic happiness. Under such circumstances the Methodist Church grew and prospered until it had large congregations throughout the region.

In addition to the itinerant preacher, Sunday Schools, and camp meetings, The American Bible Society sent agents to Texas. State and county auxiliary societies were formed. In 1839, a branch of this society was formed at Nacogdoches with Frost Thorn as its president, Haden Edwards, Kelsey H. Douglass, and William Sparks its vice presidents, Thomas J. Rusk its treasurer, Charles Gould its secretary, and David S. Kaufman and Andrew S. Hamilton its distributors.

When churches were gradually established in every community, many proclaimed themselves "union" congregations. By this they meant that the building had been erected as a project on which many persons had labored, regardless of denominational preference. In many cases a full-time pastor could not be obtained, instead ministers served several churches, visiting each at regular intervals. Perhaps a Presbyterian preacher would conduct services one Sunday, a Methodist the next, and perhaps a Baptist the next. Every churchgoer in the community attended all services whenever possible.

One of the first Protestant ministers to preach in Texas was Sumner Bacon, the pioneer of the Cumberland Presbyterian Church, who in 1832 along with Needham J. Alford held a camp meeting near the present town of Milam in Sabine County. In 1829 Bacon crossed the Sabine River at Myrick's Ferry twenty miles south of Logansport, Louisiana and from there entered Shelby County and later visited Nacogdoches. After 1832, Bacon preached and engaged in other missionary work in East Texas until the outbreak of the Texas Revolution. He enlisted in the Texas Army and participated in the Battle of San Jacinto. At the end of the war he made his home in San Augustine.

EARLY EAST TEXAS

    Bacon was preacher and evangelist rather than a church organizer and builder. He preached at camp meetings, schoolhouses, under brush arbors, and in the homes of people. The first Presbytery of the Cumberland Presbyterians in Texas met at his home in 1837 with him and two other ministers in attendance: Mitchell Smith and Amos Roark. At this meeting Richard O. Watkins[45] of Nacogdoches County, the first Cumberland Presbyterian minister ordained in Texas, was received as a candidate. In 1834, Watkins had assisted in the organization of the Watkins Settlement Presbyterian Church ten miles northeast of Nacogdoches. The second Presbytery was also held in San Augustine County and in 1843 the first Synod assembled on the camp ground near Nacogdoches. After Bacon's death in 1844, the Cumberland Presbyterian work went to pieces and was never revived.

    Cumberland Presbyterianism was never strong in the days of the Republic. By 1837 only four churches had been organized: one of which was in Sabine County and another in Nacogdoches County, and only three ministers were there to serve them.

    The area around San Augustine was also the

---

[45] Watkins was born in 1816 near Murfreesboro, Tennessee and immigrated to Texas in 1834 as a single man.

EARLY EAST TEXAS

birthplace of the Presbyterian Church (U. S. A.) in East Texas. In 1838 the Reverend Hugh Wilson,[46] a missionary of the church, organized a church with twenty-two members about four miles west of San Augustine near the community of Dwire. Wilson continued to minister to this little congregation from June to October 1838 when he departed for Independence in Washington County. Thereafter, the San Augustine church prospered under a number of ministers until the disaster of Civil War caused it to go into temporary abeyance.

Reverend Samuel Bacon organized a Cumberland Presbyterian Sunday School in Nacogdoches in 1836, and two years later Reverend Richard O. Watkins took over the school and in 1840 organized a church. However, in 1849, this congregation disbanded, and it was not until many

---

[46] Wilson was born in 1794 in Bethany, North Carolina the son of a Presbyterian minister. After being taught by the Reverend John Makemie, he attended Princeton graduating with undergraduate and seminary degrees. In 1822 he was licensed as a minister in North Carolina. He then became a missionary to Chickasaw Indians in Alabama and Mississippi. He toured Texas in 1837 and brought his family to live there the next year.

years later that the Presbyterian Church in the United States was organized and the Cumberland Presbyterian Church reorganized.

The history of the Protestant Episcopal Church in East Texas begins only after statehood. In 1848, at the urging of Frances C. Henderson, wife of James P. Henderson, the first Governor of the State of Texas, the Committee on Domestic Missions sent the Reverend Henry Sanson, an Englishman with a good education, to take up missionary work at San Augustine and Nacogdoches. At first, Sanson conducted services in the Methodist Church, the only church building in town, and later in the lower floor of the Masonic Hall.

Baptist preachers made only sporadic attempts to cross the Sabine River into Texas. In 1820, for example, Joseph E. Bays[47] came from Missouri to Sabine Parish, Louisiana where he remained for several years. During this time he preached at the home of Joseph Hinds near San Augustine, the first recorded Baptist service on Texas soil. He was arrested in 1823, but escaped and returned to

---

[47] Bays was born in North Carolina about 1786 but in 1794 moved with his family to Kentucky. At age sixteen he began preaching, and in 1804 married and moved to Missouri.

EARLY EAST TEXAS

Louisiana.

The first permanent Baptist Church in Texas was organized in 1837 in Washington-on-the-Brazos by Z. N. Morrell. Local tradition maintains that the first Baptist congregation in San Augustine County was organized in 1834 or 1835 at Hangman's Hill by a minister named Rose who went from there to Nacogdoches County. The church at Hangman's hill did not long survive. Another local account states, however, that the first Baptist Church within the limits of the old San Augustine Municipality was situated at New Hope, about five miles north of Milam in Sabine County. In any event, there was a church called Bethel in that vicinity in the early years of the Republic.

Records demonstrate that a Baptist minister held a meeting in the town of San Augustine in 1843 in the lower floor of the Masonic Hall. Attendance was good and well publicized, but no organization was forthcoming.

In 1833, Daniel Parker[48], who had just arrived

---

[48] Parker was born in Virginia in 1781, and after coming to Texas he participated in the Consultation of 1835 as a delegate from Nacogdoches and was a member of the Provisional Government. He was elected to the Congress of the Republic in 1838 but could not serve because ministers were

EARLY EAST TEXAS

in Texas from Illinois, began organizing "Two Seed" Baptist churches despite the legal ban against Protestant churches. Shortly after the end of the Texas Revolution he organized churches at Hopewell near Nacogdoches and near Palestine. He continued organizing churches in East Texas--New Bethel in Sabine County in 1838, Mt. Pleasant in Montgomery County, Fort Houston in Anderson County, Bethel in Sabine County in 1841, and Mustang Prairie and Wolf Creek whose locations are now uncertain.

In addition, Lemuel Herrin[49] and Isaac Reed[50] organized Border Church in Harrison County, Macedonia Church near Carthage, and Eight Mile Church in Harrison County. Old North Church, six miles north of Nacogdoches, was organized in 1838 by Pastor Reed. The church stands where Mrs. Massie Millard had held prayer meetings at night under the

---

barred from holding office.

[49] Herrin was born about 1800 in Benton County, Tennessee, and was ordained 1826 before coming to Texas.

[50] Reed was born June 6, 1776 in Pendleton District, South Carolina and immigrated to Texas in 1834 settling first in Nacogdoches County and later west of Carthage in Panola County.

EARLY EAST TEXAS

trees to escape possible Indian attack.

As late as 1840 there were only a dozen relatively small Baptist Churches in all of Texas. By 1843, however, Baptists and Baptist Churches were rapidly increasing their numbers in East Texas. That year the Sabine Baptist Association was organized and in some three years time boasted seven ministers, sixteen churches, and about 500 members. This association, however, soon dissolved over the missionary issue, with Reed going with the Anti-Missionaries and Herrin with the Missionaries.

The Christian Church was a relative late-comer to the Nacogdoches-San Augustine area. As early as 1824, however, the McKinney family headed by Collin McKinney located on Hickman's Prairie in present-day Bowie County in Northeast Texas. Thereafter, McKinney, Elder Moore, and Brother G. Gates organized a church which endured until 1847 when the last of the McKinney's left the area.

Council Billingsly[51] and P. F. Sullivan just prior to the outbreak of the Civil War began riding through Shelby and San Augustine Counties

---

[51] Billingsly was born in Blount County, Alabama in 1811. In 1832 he joined the Christian Church but did not come to Texas until 1858 when he settled in Shelby County eleven miles west of present-day Center which he later helped to lay out.

preaching where they could, in private homes, in brush arbors, in the open woods, or any place that they could find. They aroused intense prejudice, particularly on the part of the Methodists and Baptists; but they won many converts from the churched and the unchurched.

Two other groups of Disciples were being formed in 1836: Mansil W. Matthews and Lynn D'Spain gathered a congregation from Disciples in Alabama, Mississippi, and Tennessee and settled at Clarksville in present-day Red River County, and another group led by Dr. William Defee established a church about four miles from San Augustine. The next year Matthews and D'Spain paused for a time in Nacogdoches County where they formed another congregation of Disciples.

Even though itinerant ministers succeeded in preaching when they desired in the years proceeding independence, nevertheless formal religious services were rare events. Thus, many of the children of the early settlers who came of age while Texas was an independent nation had little or no knowledge of formal religion, nor had many of their elders heard a sermon for several years. Skepticism was prevalent among the lawyers and doctors, but many individuals who had been active church members found it difficult to maintain their piety in frontier Texas.

Lack of intercourse with fellow believers, the

excesses of frontier towns, and license provoked by aftermaths of the war were antireligious forces at work throughout the new republic. The Christian tenets of peace, love, forgiveness, salvation, and redemption did not appeal to many of the self-reliant frontier individualists who early came to Texas. Observation of the Sabbath was not common. Church buildings were scarce. A religious census dated 1845 indicated that not more than one-eighth of the white population were members, active or nominal, of Texas churches. Protestantism dominated the religious scene. Methodist, Baptist, Presbyterian, Catholic, and Protestant Episcopal churches had the greatest numerical strength, although some minor sects did exist in limited numbers.

EARLY EAST TEXAS

CHAPTER NINE

LAW AND JUSTICE

When Anglo American settlers immigrated to Texas in the years before independence, they encountered a legal system with which they were not at all familiar. The Spanish-Mexican system was based on Roman legal precepts and known to them as civil law, while the American system was derived from English legal axioms known to them as common law.

After the Declaration of Independence in 1836, the Texans adopted a constitution for the Republic of Texas, and in it they made it clear that the common law was now supreme over the pre-existing civil law. From the law and custom of Spanish-Mexican days, they, nevertheless, borrowed legal concepts and incorporated them into a unique blend of both legal systems.

Complex Legal System

From the law and customs of Spanish-Mexican colonial times, Anglo-American lawmakers in the days following Texas independence combined them with the legal concepts they had brought with

EARLY EAST TEXAS

them from the United States to fashion a complex legal system. They retained colonial civil law concepts concerning land titles and land law in general, debtor relief, marital relations, adoption, water and other mineral rights, and judicial procedures.

Spanish and Mexican grants created property rights over some 27,000,000 acres of Texas land. Post-war lawmakers expressly guaranteed that rights would be protected. Among other property principles retained were those dealing with mineral rights. Spanish civil law vested title to all minerals in the King, that is, in the Spanish Monarchy. The Republic of Texas succeeded to that title following the Revolution, and it was not until 1866 that the State of Texas relinquished title to any and all minerals beneath the surface of its lands to the current and future landowners.

The civil law dealing with riparian rights (water rights) Texas constitution makers also found congenial. That system decreed that supplies of water were to be divided by the process of those with access taking turns as the supply afforded from a ditch owned and controlled by the community. The common law had guaranteed riparian owners the full and undiminished flow of streams that passed thorough their property and thus precluded extensive irrigation projects which allowed removal of water

EARLY EAST TEXAS

from those streams. Texas law combined provisions of the two systems to provide that unappropriated water could be diverted for irrigation purposes and that the first appropriator had a right to only as much water as needed for domestic purposes.

Other property rights concepts such as those concerning debtor relief were also retained. Among them, the homestead exemption, was perhaps the most prominent. That doctrine specified that a married man was entitled to have his homestead exempt from debts except for repairs and taxes on it and along with it personal property such as clothing and furniture. It further safeguarded his livestock and some rural acreage thus allowing him to continue to earn a livelihood for himself and his family. Moreover, civil law did not permit imprisonment for non-payment of debt as did the common law. A man's wages could not be garnished (attached) for debt and his tools could not be confiscated for non-payment. All of these concepts found their way into the fundamental law of the Republic of Texas and later the State of Texas.

Under common law rules the right of females to own and control property was highly restricted. In most circumstances any property owned by a female became the undisputed property of her spouse or guardian. The Spanish civil law system of community property apparently appealed to frontier American notions of equality for the common law was sharply modified by the civil law concept in Texas.

Community property provisions in Texas law decreed that at the time of marriage, unless otherwise agreed, husbands and wives became equal partners in property subsequently acquired with the profits of the partnership equally divided on the dissolution of the marriage and with the husband as temporary manager of the partnership. Spouses could maintain separate property, and as a general rule property owned at the time of marriage and property acquired after the marriage by inheritance or gift remained separate property. In certain circumstances a wife could manage her separate property without interference from her husband and could enter into contracts with him where her property was concerned.

A further area where Spanish civil law profoundly affected legal rights in Texas centered on paternal-filial relations. The Anglo American common law system in the early years of the Nineteenth Century recognized a system of guardian and ward for those children whose parents were deceased but legal adoption was not permitted. It also stipulated that adult females should also have guardians appointed to manage their property. Legal systems derived from Roman law including Spanish civil law permitted even encouraged a system of legal adoption and Texas lawmakers never took action to repeal the system.

EARLY EAST TEXAS

During the same time frame the common law system in place in the southern states of America permitted the parent to will his entire estate to one of his heirs, traditionally the first-born son (known as primogeniture), leaving all others without inheritance from the estate. Spanish law prohibited the process, instead it adopted the contrary process of forced heirship whereby the testator's estate had to be divided among all his heirs.

The English legal system had spawned a variety of courts and an accompanying variety of legal procedures. Most prominent among those courts were those applying the rules of common law and those relying on the concepts of equity. Civil law never developed those distinctions. Thus, when Anglo americans came to Texas, notably the lawyers among them, they discovered courts that combined both law and equity. Moreover, common law procedures were grounded on a practice of pleading by writ, while the Spanish-Mexican system employed a method of pleading by petition and answer. The much simpler Spanish-Mexican system appealed to frontier lawyers, and they readily combined it with the common law-equity systems to create a mixed system whereby Spanish-Mexican practice governed the proceedings (pleadings) while the Anglo American furnished the rule of decisions.

Although civil law concepts made some

EARLY EAST TEXAS

inroads, Texas constitution framers were adamant in proclaiming that the common law as understood and practiced "back in the states" was the basis of all law in the Republic of Texas. Where the law was silent or where civil law and common conflicted, the common law would prevail unless constitutional provisions specifically provided otherwise.

A special case in the development of a legal system in Texas was the place of the institution of slavery. Spanish colonial law recognized slavery, but at the same time it prohibited the slave trade and proclaimed that slaves born within the jurisdiction of the empire at age fourteen should be freed. The national colonization law contained ambiguous provisions relating to slavery, but its framers probably intended to prohibit the importation of slaves by colonists even for their own use. However, that was not how it was interpreted in colonial Texas.

The 1827 Constitution of the State of Coahulia y Texas recognized existing slavery within the state, permitted the introduction of additional slaves for six months after its publication, but declared that children born of slaves thereafter should be free. The state congress enacted legislation permitting the buying and selling of slaves within the state and allowed "hiring" slaves to others than their owners for periods of sixty years. Nevertheless, legally there was no way to import slaves. Consequently, immigration by southern planters whose way of life was dependent on the utilization of slave labor almost ceased.

The state congress responded in 1828 by enacting legislation that recognized and honored "contracts" made in foreign countries between potential settlers and servants or hirelings. In consideration of the master's promise to take the slave to Texas with him where he would be free, the slaves promised to work for the master for the rest of his life. The 1830 national immigration statute struck a blow at the institution by recognizing existing slavery but prohibiting future importation of slaves and their American masters. An 1832 state statute struck further at the institution. It provided that immigrants would be subject to existing and all future laws relating to slavery and that "labor contracts" were limited to a period of only ten years.

Theory and practice tended to be at variance, at least in Mexican Texas. In spite of first Spanish and then later Mexican government attempts to discourage the existence of slavery in frontier Texas, slave labor became increasingly important in the agricultural economy of East Texas. In 1825 Stephen F. Austin's 1,347 colonists owned 443 slaves, and a decade later Mexican estimates placed the number of slaves in the Department of the Brazos at some 1,000 out of a total population of ten times that number. At the same time the proportion of slaves in the Department of

EARLY EAST TEXAS

Nacogdoches was approximately the same.

In 1836 when the Constitution of the Republic of Texas legalized the institution of slavery, the total population of the Republic was estimated at 30,000 Anglos, 4,000 Mexicans, and 5,000 slaves, but by 1847, there were 100,000 Anglos in the state who owned some 40,000 slaves. From 1835 on the eve of the Revolution the proportion of slaves was estimated at about twelve percent, but by 1850 when the first federal census was taken it had risen to some twenty-seven percent.

The greatest part of this influx of settlers consisted of Southern planters who were enticed by the promise of cheap or even free land, and they naturally brought their capital in the form of slaves with them. Slaves were not, however, spread evenly throughout the settled portion of Texas. They were confined almost entirely to eastern plantations where sugar cane, tobacco, rice, and cotton were the predominant crops.

Although most Texans owned few if any slaves, most of them approved the legalization of the institution. They believed it was essential that slavery be defended and perpetuated for both the spiritual and economic welfare of the slave. They were also convinced that the more profitable forms of agriculture could be carried on only with slave labor, and thus they were anxious to acquire at least a few slaves to assist them in bettering their economic position.

One of the most unusual innovations adopted by framers of the Constitution of the Republic of Texas was that concerning ministers of the gospel. It proclaimed that ministers being by their profession dedicated to God and the care of men's souls should not be diverted from their duties and functions, they were not eligible to serve as the nation's president or as a member of its congress.

A French version of Roman Law known as the Napoleonic Code was the basis of the legal system in nearby Louisiana, and in 1835 provisions of that code became the rule in all cases of sequestration, attachment, or arrest and would govern all writs dealing with those actions. Sequestration involved a mandate issued by a court ordering the sheriff, in certain specified cases, to take possession and retain a thing in another's possession until a court decision could determined who should have legal possession. Attachment was concerned with the process of seizing persons or property and placing them within then custody of a court to assure the appearance of persons or providing security for debts, costs, or prevention of alienation of property. In the Louisiana Code arrest was a means whereby the creditor is secured in the debt while his suit is pending or to compel the debtor to give security for his appearance after judgment.

EARLY EAST TEXAS

Confronted by conflicting legal systems, frontier notions of law and justice, the absence of law schools and scarcity of law books the approach of Texans to the adoption of a legal system at the time of the creation of the Republic was necessarily a pragmatic one. Out of inclination and necessity they fashioned a system that discarded whenever possible intricate procedures and retained those elements that had the most appeal to their frontier sense of fairness and justice.

Legal Practice and Practitioners

The unusually diversified system of law that made up the Texas legal system after 1836 confronted the legal profession at a time when its general standards of training and practice were low. Truly competent lawyers were, therefor, in great demand. Lawyers of all degrees of competence flocked to the new nation where the insecurity of land titles promised lucrative litigation, and expectations of increasing land values stimulated the promise of acquired wealth. While a distinct minority of them were highly trained and eminently qualified, most fell far short of that distinction.

On the whole, however, law was a highly regarded profession which frequently created opportunity to gain community influence and launched successful political and military careers. Financial returns, on the other hand, were moderate at best and in times of depression were meager indeed. As a result, few lawyers engaged exclusively in the practice of law. The more successful held most of the important political positions, operated plantations, and became large landowners. The less successful often taught school, preached, edited newspapers, promoted town development, farmed, and became innkeepers.

To engage in the practice of law, an individual had to pass an examination conducted by a court or under its direction. The customary procedure in early Texas, in preparing for the bar examination, was to become an apprentice of an established lawyer. The usual period of study was three years, but in the Republic tended to be somewhat less. The apprentice read his supervisor's law books, learned how to write legal documents, and generally acted as his clerk and janitor.

After several months of study, the applicant was examined by a committee of three members of the bar appointed by the district judge. If satisfied, the committee recommended that the applicant be issued a license, and the court did so after a modest fee was paid and a solemn oath taken. Perhaps surprisingly few of those licensed conducted themselves in a manner to bring serious condemnation of their profession, and those who did not where usually viewed with tolerance.

Few lawyers possessed more than a few law books, and a law library of more than a score of books was rare. The result was that many lawyers were poorly educated and relied on common sense rather than legal citations when arguing their cases.

In sharp contrast to the poorly educated frontier lawyers that made up the bulk of those in practice in republican Texas, the leadership of its bar included some very talented individuals and even a few with genuine claims to distinction. Thomas J. Rusk of Nacogdoches and his partners J. Pinckney Henderson and Kenneth L. Anderson of San Augustine, George W. Terrell, William B. Ochiltree, and Royal T. Wheeler also of San Augustine, all members of the East Texas Bar were very able practitioners who rendered valuable services to the Republic. The San Antonio and Brazoria Bars contained an extremely high level of legal talent as well. Anderson, for example, was the last Vice President of the Republic of Texas.

The Bar of San Augustine unquestionably deserved its reputation for strength and brilliance in oratory and rhetoric and solidity of legal learning and acuteness of reasoning. Two of them became Chief Justices of the Supreme Court of Texas while others were members of the appellate court bench. In addition, nearly all the district judges and district attorneys for the Fifth District practiced in San Augustine.[52]

The courts of San Augustine played an important part in molding the mixture of English common law, Spanish civil law, and the Code Napoleon into the foundation of Texas law. They were instrumental in adapting that mixture to the needs and requirements of the people of their region and all of the nation.

Courts and Judges

The court system of the Republic of Texas consisted of a simple framework very similar to that in Tennessee and other southern states of the time. A Supreme Court, a small number of District Courts, a larger number of County Courts, and a rather numerous collection of Justice Courts constituted its parts.

To replace the colonial Spanish-Mexican system of alcalde's courts and cannon (Church) courts, in 1835 the Provisional Government of Texas mandated the selection of two judges for each

---

[52] Appendix III contains name and other data on the East Texas Bar during the time of the Republic of Texas.

municipality, one designated as first judge and the other second judge. They had jurisdiction over all crimes recognized by common law and their procedures generally followed common law practices. Judges who served in the East Texas municipalities during this time included: John Forbes and Radford Berry in Nacogdoches, John G. Love and W. N. Seiger in San Augustine, Emery Raines and James English in Tenaha (Shelby), and George W. Smith and James Mott in Bevil (Jasper). This temporary arrangement was terminated in 1836 and 1837 when the courts created by the Constitution of the Republic of Texas were organized.

The court system of the Republic was headed by a Supreme Court which was composed of a Chief Justice and all of the District Judges.[53] A majority of the district judges along with the Chief Justice constituted a quorum. The District Judges therefore were also styled Associate Justices of the Supreme Court. These judges were elected by a joint session of both houses of the Congress for terms of four years and were eligible for reelection.

The Supreme Court could only hear criminal and civil cases on appeal but could hear appeals from

---

[53] Appendix II provides names and other data concerning Chief Justices and District (Associate Justices) Judges.

any court in the Republic. All such trials were required to be de novo (that is, entirely new trials) upon both the record compiled by the trial court and the facts of the case having been agreed on by the parties or certified by the trial judge. A Chief Justice and four Associate Justices were elected in 1837, but the court did not hold its first session until early in 1840. Although legal historians point out that the court's decisions contained few references to legal authorities, they commend the vigor of those decisions.

In 1836 the Republic's Congress divided the nation into four districts and established a District Court in each. In 1838, a fifth district was added, and still later, in 1840, a sixth and seventh districts were created. Each District Court was presided over by a District Judge who was required to be or become a resident in his district where he was to hold session of his court twice each year in each county included in the district.

District Courts had original jurisdiction over civil suits where the amount in controversy exceeded $100 unless that jurisdiction was expressly assigned to another court and over criminal trials involving treason, murder, and other felonies and misdemeanors unless assigned to another court. Their judges were authorized to issue writs of habeas corpus, mandamus, and injunctions. Later their jurisdiction was increased to include cases in equity and admiralty law, divorce and separate maintenance cases, and all appeals from justice courts that had earlier been appealed to county courts.

Their decisions could be appealed to the Supreme Court in civil cases if the amount involved was more than $300 and in all criminal cases. Jury trials were guaranteed in all civil and criminal cases, and facts as determined by juries could not be altered. Cases were initiated by a petition setting forth the petitioner's claims or the crime for which he stood accused.

Also in 1836, the Congress established a County Court for each of the counties of the Republic. It was composed of a Chief Justice elected by a joint ballot of both houses of Congress for a term of four years and two Associate Justices selected by a majority of the county's justices of the peace each year. A majority of the justices was necessary to form a quorum. They were required to hold sessions four times each year at the county seat.

County Courts were given jurisdiction over all civil cases involving $100 or more, along with the District Courts; but no case involving title to land could be tried in a county court. Their decision in civil cases involving $200 or more could be appealed to the District Court. Litigants involved in cases before the county court could demand a jury trial if the amount at issue was $21 or more. The Chief Justice of the County Court was made a probate judge with authority to validate wills, grant letters of administration of estates, appoint guardians; and in conjunction with his Associate Justices examine and settle accounts of executors, administrators, and guardians of estates.

In addition to their judicial duties, County Courts were required to obtain and maintain a courthouse and a jail at the county seat. They were also required to layout, discontinue, or maintain the county's public roads. In 1839, however, a statute enacted by the Congress limiting the basic functions to the County Court to exercise of the powers of probate, conservation of the peace, supervision of county roads and county revenues; all other judicial functions were transferred to the District Courts.

Then, in 1841, election by the voters of the county became the method of choosing Chief Justices; and in 1844 the County Court was reorganized to consist of the Chief Justice and a four-member Board of Commissioners all elected by county voters. The same 1844 statute eliminated Associate Justices of the County from dealing with probate matters.

Statutes mandated the creation of two justice courts for each precinct in a county. They were presided over by Justices of the Peace elected by the voters of the precinct for two-year terms. They were empowered to keep the peace, see to it that individuals appeared to answer lesser criminal charges, to commit to jail those who did not comply with judicial orders, to indict all persons suspected of any crime, and to issue search warrants for stolen goods.

They were courts of record with jurisdiction over any civil case which did not involve more than $100, but all decision in civil cases involving more than $20 could be appealed to the County Court for a trial de novo. Along with the Chief Justice, Justices of the Peace later became a board of commissioners to superintend roads, highways, ferries, and bridges and supervise treatment of the poor.

In 1837, Justices of the Peace, ordained Ministers of the Gospel, District Judges and Chief Justices of the County were authorized to celebrate marriages between those legally permitted to marry. Males under fourteen and females under twelve years of age were not permitted to marry.

Two years later a six-man jury was created to assist the Justice of the peace in suits to recover articles of personal property, torts, trespass, and other legal injuries resulting in damages where the amount of damages did not exceed $100.

Clearly, the court system of the Republic passed through a decade of trial and error. By the time the Republic was annexed to the United States, however, a mature system had emerged, many facets of which remain in place in the court system of modern Texas.

Those individuals who held the offices of District Judge or Chief Justice of the Supreme Court were, taken as a whole, men of talent, learning, and distinction who were worthy of the name of jurists. Individuals who served as Chief Justice of a County Court and Justice of the Peace were rarely members of the legal profession, and the offices were most certainly not considered as full-time occupations. Available evidence indicates that these officers were most commonly engaged in farming, but merchants, physicians, ministers, and surveyors were relatively common. Less than three percent were lawyers, while some were blacksmiths, millers, ranchers, carpenters, tavern keepers, hotel keepers, and ginners.

The East Texas Bar furnished a number of distinguished judges of the Republic of Texas bench. One of the Chief Justices of the Supreme Court was Thomas Jefferson Rusk of Nacogdoches, the third Chief Justice (1838-1840). Rusk was a native of the Pendleton District of South Carolina who in 1835 settled in Nacogdoches County. During the Texas Revolution he served as a contractor, brigadier general, and inspector general for the Texas Army. In 1836, he was named Secretary of War of the Republic and represented the Nacogdoches Municipality in the

EARLY EAST TEXAS

Constitutional Convention.

He represented Nacogdoches in the Second Congress (1837-1838), commanded a force of 600 men in quelling the Cordovan Rebellion in 1838 and a regiment of troops in the Cherokee War in 1839, becoming Major General of Militia in 1843. In 1845 was elected to represent Nacogdoches in the Constitutional Convention where he served as its president. He was chosen by the First Legislature of the State of Texas to serve as one of the two United States Senators from the new state, where he served from 1846 to 1856, having been chosen president pro tem during his second term.

When courts were first established in 1837, almost all of the territory east of the Trinity River was included in the First District, but three years later the Republic was redistricted and Houston, San Augustine, and Nacogdoches Counties were placed in a new Fifth District, while Jefferson, Jasper, Sabine, and Shelby were included in a new Sixth District.[54]

More than half of the judges who served the First, Fifth, and Sixth Districts were East Texans. Among the most notable of these were who lived in San Augustine were Shelby Corzine, George W.

---

[54] See Appendix II for a list of the East Texans who served as judges in these districts.

EARLY EAST TEXAS

Terrell, and Richardson A. Scurry. Corzine had been one of the commissioners who helped determined the boundary between Texas and the United States and had been a member of the Congress of the Republic. He had the distinction of presiding over the only treason trial held in the Republic's courts.

Terrell had been District Attorney for the First District, Secretary of State of the Republic, Attorney General of the Republic, Indian Commissioner for the Republic, and charges d'affairs to France, Great Britain, and Spain. Judge Scurry moved to Clarksville in Red River County before being chosen as a District Judge.

In addition, William B. Ochiltree and Royal T. Wheeler lived in both San Augustine and Nacogdoches Counties. Ochiltree had been Secretary of the Treasury of the Republic and its Adjutant General. He also became a delegate to the Constitutional Convention of 1845 and a member of the Texas State Legislature. Royal Wheeler had been District Attorney of the Fifth District, and later became an Associate Justice of the Texas State Supreme Court before becoming its Chief Justice.

The unsettled conditions of the country demanded that these district judges be firm and tactful, if not always well versed in the law of the land. The problems in human relations confronting them required of them that they be rugged, sensible, and not too insistent on legal formalities than that they be well versed in the technicalities of the law.

In the time of the Republic Nacogdoches County had three County Chief Justices with Charles S. Taylor being perhaps the most prominent.[55] Taylor had represented Nacogdoches County in the Consultation of 1832, and the Convention of 1836, Alcalde of San Augustine County, and Nacogdoches County Treasurer.

Four men served as Chief Justices of Sabine County of those Parker was perhaps the most distinguished. He became a member of the Sabine County Land Commission and a member of the Senate of the State of Texas. Archibald W. O. Hicks was the best known of the four men who became Chief Justices of Shelby County. He later represented the county in the Convention of 1845 and became the Judge of the Fifth Judicial District of the State of Texas.

In all, six men became Chief Justices of San Augustine County. Edwin O. LeGrand and William McFarland were perhaps the most prominent among them. LeGrand represented the county in the Convention of 1836 and was Inspector General of the Texas Army. McFarland surveyed the town site for

---

[55] See Appendix II for a list of all the East Texas County Chief Justices.

EARLY EAST TEXAS

San Augustine, represented Ayish Bayou in the Consultation of 1832 and later served as Alcalde for the San Augustine Municipality.

With each county divided into as many justice precincts as "was convenient," the number of justices of the peace varied from county to county. Nacogdoches County voters, for example, elected some sixty-four in the days of the Republic; thirty-three were chosen in Sabine County, fifty-nine in Shelby County, and thirty-nine in San Augustine County.

By far most of the men who were elected justices of the peace in East Texas were local farmers who were honest, upstanding members of their communities. With little or no formal education nor knowledge of the law, they dealt with small claims and minor breaches of the peace with common sense and inherent wisdom. A few of them, however, went on to become distinguished public officers. John H. Reagan of Nacogdoches County was twice elected a Nacogdoches County Justice of the Peace, Chief Justice of Kaufman County, a state representative from Henderson County, a state District Judge for two terms, a United States Congressman, a delegate to the Secession Convention of 1861, Postmaster General and Secretary of the Treasury of the Confederacy, a United State Senator, chairman of the Texas Railroad Commission, and delegate to the Texas Conventions

EARLY EAST TEXAS

of 1866 and 1875.

Stephen W. Blount of San Augustine County was a delegate to the Constitutional Convention of 1836, County Clerk of San Augustine County, and District Clerk of the First Judicial District of the Republic. A third man, Ephraim M. Daggett of Shelby County was a veteran of the Mexican War, the Moderator Regulator feud, and a state representative.

Suits to establish titles to land and other property and to collect debts dominated the civil dockets of the courts, and many lawyers specialized in land law. Nevertheless, practically all attorneys maintained a criminal as well as a civil practice, and surviving court records demonstrate their consistent success in obtaining decisions of not prosecuted (nolle proseaqui), quashed indictments, hung juries, case continuances, and acquittals. Their initial step in handling a case often involved obtaining a sympathetic jury who would not be too interested in the intricacies of the law but in the oratory of the lawyer. Because of their record in winning cases for the defendant, criminal lawyers were seen as public benefactors, and they, as a group, were highly regarded in their communities.

The Texas practice of settling differences by personal encounters, whether by fighting, shooting, stabbing, or dueling made the task of public prosecutors difficult. Convictions for most serious crimes were followed by moderate sentences. Convictions in the most serious criminal cases were hard to come by because juries tended to give serious consideration to pleas of self-defense, unbearable provocation, and severity of punishment.

Court records reveal that indictments for gambling were more numerous than for any other crime, but less than fifteen percent of those indictments resulted in convictions. Professional gamblers were numerous in some localities, and their games quite often produced altercations. Theft, particularly theft of livestock, was looked upon by many as a more serious crime than murder and convictions brought with them harsh punishments such as whipping and branding.

Fourteen offenses were punishable by death, but the crimes for which punishment of incarceration for more than one year were very few. Those prosecutions where the punishment was deemed too harsh were rarely brought to a guilty verdict. The laxity of law enforcement often gave rise to vigilance committees and occasional lynching.

As a rule, the desperadoes, gamblers, and gunmen tended to flock together in boom towns and in other areas favorable to their activities, while total lawlessness was in play only in the period immediately following the Revolution when fighting spirit still ran high and law enforcement agencies were in their infancy. At the same time limits on immigration were nonexistent allowing all sorts of individuals to leave the United States and head for Texas. The great majority of newcomers were hardy homesteaders who were essentially a law-abiding people.

CHAPTER TEN

PHYSICIANS AND MEDICINES

Anglo Americans who settled in colonial and post-Revolutionary Texas frequently boasted that this region was the most healthful in America, but a careful study of physicians and their medications does not confirm their claims. Records indicate that cholera, for example, took a heavy toll in lives. In 1833 and 1834 epidemics laid waste to the Brazoria, Goliad, Nacogdoches, and San Antonio areas. Mexican officials urged settlers to take precautionary measures, including cleanup campaigns, copper amulets for neckwear, and water from boiled peyote cactuses with a little lime and a few drops of laudanum added. Epidemics returned again in 1849, 1850, and 1852 with widespread loss of life, while in 1846 an epidemic, probably typhus, killed scores in New Braunfels and Fredricksburg.

In addition to the persistent epidemics, people suffered from other ailments: chills and fever, inflamation of the eyes, rheumatism, biliousness, measles, whooping cough, and small pox. Claims for sure cures and nostrums were widespread and extravagant, and general stores were well stocked with patent medicines ranging from cancer cures to cough remedies.

Long before those Anglo Americans began filtering into the Spanish province of Texas first and later the Mexican state two classes of individuals treated the sick and preformed primitive surgery: the Franciscan missionary priests and the local barber. The Nacogdoches Archives record that in 1795 the settlement's lone barber died and the people of the community searched avidly for a replacement.

A Royal Order dated 1777 demonstrates that some surgeons resided in the province. That order required them to attend any person wounded by violence or by accident who might summon them or who might go to their home before notifying the authorities. But as late as 1780 the provincial governor was notified that a terrible smallpox epidemic had broken out in the Presidio at La Bahia (Goliad), that there was no medicine to be had, and that there was no one to properly administer if any existed.

Physicians

Five years later, Yldefonso Rey, a recent arrival, had displayed the ability as a good barber, a bleeder, tooth extractor, and surgeon.[56] By the early

---

[56] This may be the same barber-surgeon who died in Nacogdoches ten years later.

EARLY EAST TEXAS

years of the Eighteenth Century, a few physicians of average ability had been dispatched to Texas by Spanish authorities. They settled, for the most part, in the San Antonio area. But Spanish-born Dr. Federico Zervan, a physician and surgeon, had established a provisional hospital in Coahuila in an old mission. Local officials complained that Dr. Zervan was inactive, inefficient, and without zeal in carring for patients. Although the doctor was upheld by a subsequent investigation, he never quite lived down the scandal. In 1807, he was replaced as head of the hospital by Dr. Jayme Garzo, another Spanish-born physician.

German-born Dr. Agustin Guillermo de Spangerberg who arrived in Bexar in 1793 was only twenty-eight years of age. He was a native of Strassburg in the Province of Alsace who could speak English and German, but not Spanish. After a brief sojourn in San Antonio, the Provincial Governor sent him to Coahuila. These and all other early physicians dealt with smallpox, malaria, and other diseases as best they could under frontier conditions.

Between 1821 and 1836 the Mexican government attempted, without much success, to continue the medical efforts of the Spanish. In the 1830s in East Texas, however, as more and more Anglo Americans entered the region, a few physicians immigrated with them. The 1835 Mexican Census indicated that at least one, Dr. Samuel Stivers a native of New Jersey, was practicing in the San Augustine Municipality, but he later moved his practice to Nacogdoches. In the nearby Nacogdoches Municipality Drs. Joseph and John Hertz, Joseph Milgeson, and Lemuel B. Brown appear in the 1835 Mexican Census. The Hertz brothers were natives of Hanover, Germany; but biographical information for Drs. Brown and Milgeson has not been preserved.

Earlier, in 1830, Dr. Nicholas Descomp Labadie, a Canadian-born physician, resided for a short time in Nacogdoches before proceeding to San Felipe;[57] in 1834 Dr. Jesse Korn arrived and set up a practice; and about the same time Dr. Joseph

---

[57] In 1859, Labadie, then a resident of Galveston, published an account of the Battle of San Jacinto in the Texas Almanac of that year alleging that Colonel John Forbes of Nacogdoches, Commissary General of the Texas Army, had murdered a helpless Spanish woman during the battle and in addition embezzled funds due the participants. The account resulted in a well-publicized libel suit initiated in the Nacogdoches District Court the following year. The suit was dismissed six years later without a decision being handed down. Forbes later became an early mayor of the City of Nacogdoches.

EARLY EAST TEXAS

Whitcomb also came to the municipality. These and other early Anglo physicians encountered the same diseases as the Spanish and made use of the same remedies. By 1830 the San Antonio town council required all children be vaccinated, but there is no indication that the East Texas municipalities followed suit.

The 1850 U. S. Census identified twelve physicians practicing in Nacogdoches County, ten in San Augustine County, eight in Sabine County, and seven in Shelby County[58]. For each of the four counties the ratio of physicians to total populations was about 400 to one. Because of the "horse and buggy" modes of transportation and the distances involved, each well-settled community within the county tended to have at least one resident physician.

Doctors were often well respected community leaders. For example, Nacogdoches physician James Harper Starr, a graduate of a medical college in Ohio, served as Secretary of Treasury in 1839 and President of the Nacogdoches Board of Land Commissioners[59];

---

[58] A list of these early physicians may be found in Appendix V.

[59] In 1837, an act of the Congress of the Republic provided for the creation of a general land office for the nation. In addition, in each county a board of land

EARLY EAST TEXAS

and another Nacogdoches doctor, Robert Anderson Irion, a graduate of Transylvania College in Kentucky, was a member of the Congress of the Republic and Secretary of State 1837-1838. Most were not well informed of the latest scientific developments in their profession, but they gained respect by attention to duty and by the long and difficult trips they endured over bad roads to attend to the sick. They frequently added to their somewhat meager incomes by selling drugs, practicing law, farming, preaching, selling general mercantile items, and editing newspapers.

A scattered few had excellent educational backgrounds and training. For the most part, most had obtained their medical knowledge and training through the apprentice system of "reading medicine" under the supervision of a local doctor and perhaps attendance on lectures at a medical school back in the states. With a few exceptions, they did not have access to the medical journals of the times nor to well

---

commissioners of three members would be appointed by joint action of both houses of Congress. The board would be charged with the duty of granting land certificates to citizens who were entitled to headrights.

Headrights were grants of land to heads of families and single men as a bonus for settling in Texas before and for a time after the Texas Revolution.

stocked medical libraries.

    Impostors often acquired the title of doctor of medicine by the simple process of immigrating to Texas and "hanging out their shingles." There was nothing to prevent any person who believed himself competent from proclaiming himself a physician, because no effective organization of physicians existed, and the efforts of the national government under the leadership of Dr. Ashbel Smith to restrict the practice of medicine to qualified practitioners were largely abortive and ineffectual.

    These conditions meant that medical charlatans often called "quacks" were present in the Republic. Nevertheless, court records provide no evidence that they were ever prosecuted for incompetence or practicing medicine without a license.

    In the time of the Republic physician's fees were usually $5.00 per call ($10.00 after nine o'clock at night). The financial rewards from the practice of medicine were generally disappointing for ordinary practitioners. Bills for medical attention were difficult to collect, and a Texas doctor with an estate of more than $2,500 was rare, much of his estate was made up of unpaid or partially paid bills.

    There were few dentists in the Republic, teeth were generally treated or extracted by untrained relatives or by family physicians. Doctors often advertised that along with their medical and surgical practice, they would extract teeth.

Some Texas doctors were competent surgeons, but, in the absence of anesthetics, even the hands of the most competent practitioners, were harrowing experiences for patients who were often tied or held down. In emergencies, when trained surgical assistance was not available, laymen treated patients and preformed operations.

Medical Practice

East Texas doctors visited the homes of their patients when summoned carrying their instruments and medicines with them in pill bags or other pouches that could be easily conveyed on horseback or in a buggy. On occasion they stayed for several days and nights with one patient.

They had recourse to a relatively wide variety of drugs with which to treat the illnesses they encountered. The compounded their own liquid medicines and filled capsules. Stores also stocked an assortment of patent medicines, some of which proclaiming extravagant claims. In addition to purchasing and administering dubious packaged cures, laymen often became adept at bleeding, blistering, and the application of poultices. Most physicians administered calomel[60] at the first sign of fever, quinine for chills, ipecac in cases of croup, salts and gum camphor for baby's colic, and plasters of Burgandy pitch for weakness of the back. Malaria treatments included calomel, mustard-seed plasters, castor oil, salts of senna, and quinine.

Bleeding, sweating, vomiting, and purging were standard treatments for a variety of complaints. Before doctors were called to treat a patient, home remedies were often resorted to including flour mixed with the inner bark of ash trees for treatment of liver and bowel problems, flour and willow bark for a tonic, and a brew of green gourds as an emetic. Spring tonics were widely administered, notably sulphur and molasses and sassafras tea.

One pioneer physician touted such household and herb cures as tansy roots and yarrow and catnip, and rue and balm and other bitter herbs for the relief of suffering. Tobacco juice, gun powder and vinegar, brandy and salt, alum, and a drink made from the bark of the black ash tree were recommended as antidotes for snake bite.

Many early settlers were naively superstitious

---

[60] Calomel was also known as mercurous chloride, it was a white, tasteless powder used primarily as a purgative and fungicide in modern times.

and placed much faith in incantations and the like. For this reason, doctors often resorted to endowing bread pills, colored water, and other placebos with Latin names in order to reassure the weak and depressed. Slaves frequently had to be forced to take calomel and castor oil believing that calomel was compounded from the bones of dead persons and castor oil extracted from their tissues. Dread of night air was widespread and fresh air when sleeping was avoided. On the whole, however, ordinary persons were not far behind the majority of their doctors in medical knowledge and practice, for both suffered from the backward state of medical science.

    An attempt to organize a state medical society occurred in 1853 at a state convention at Austin but little was accomplished to elevate standards and regularize entrance into the profession. Not until 1869 in the face of mounting deaths from smallpox and yellow fever was an effective organization created.

CHAPTER ELEVEN

LIFESTYLES

During the formative years a unique lifestyle evolved in East Texas and to a large extent throughout the entire region. It emerged as a blend of Spanish colonial experience, Anglo American individualism, frontier conditions in the area, and a nationalism generated during the decade of independence. These elements magnified by an exaggerated sense of self-importance and group territoriality. As in the case of many frontiers, it was made up of an armed society with its codes and courtesies, an incipient feudalism, a touchy sense of independence, and a determined self-reliance.

Out of these elements emerged a Texas patriotism not based on institutions of government or idealism, but on the long struggle to gain possession of the land. This territoriality sprang from the reaction of men and women from one culture or civilization into a new and different set of conditions, where they felt they were beset by enemies they despised. Texans emerged from this struggle with a unique historical memory. That memory contains cultural myths influenced by events such as the Alamo, Goliad, and San Jacinto.

EARLY EAST TEXAS

Frontier Texas attracted a group of nonconformists personified by its first national leader, Sam Houston. Many of those individuals, perhaps most of them, gained a reputation for toughness that repelled the more timid prospective immigrants and drove such individuals out or away. A visitor to the area in 1846 concluded that Texans were the most independent people under the whole canopy of heaven.

Some of the more predominant characteristics of this rampant individualism included a sense of separate independence on the part of individuals, a system of armed neutrality among them, a resentment of real or imaged encroachments on personal rights, a readiness to settle disputes without resort to law, and an acceptance of persons regardless of their past history. Their crude sense of individuality manifested itself in imaginative, exaggerated humor--tall tales, yarns, and bigness and bestness of all things Texan.

Amusements

Swearing was honed to a fine "art" that required highly individualized, creative imaginations. This was seen by many as a passion for "freedom of speech" and its downside was it tendency to provoke fights and duels. Turbulence escalated after 1836 to the point that most indictments in distinct courts involved charges of assault and battery, affray (a brawl or noisy fight), assault with intent to kill, and murder. Moreover, many other altercations were not made the subject of legal action.

Many of these encounters resulted from the widespread custom of wearing Bowie knives and pistols. Some affrays ended in fatalities which the lack of adequate law enforcement agencies combined with the presence of ruffians who often drew into fights persons who normally would never have been involved. When a "bad" man died in a clash, the public reaction was that justice had been satisfied; but when an ordinary law-abiding individual was the victim the reaction was quite different, on occasion resulting in vigilante action.

Few duels were fought in the decades proceeding independence, but thereafter both fighting and dueling were more frequent. Adherence to the principles of the Code of Honor by individuals in the Republic of Texas, especially persons in military or political life, was widespread. After 1840, however, resort to dueling declined sharply, perhaps because that year the Congress of the Republic enacted a stringent law banning the practice.

Duels and brawls also declined as an outgrowth of the impact of the Panic of 1837 on the nation's economy. The fever of speculation in townsites and other land schemes had reached

EARLY EAST TEXAS

epidemic proportions by 1836, but the Panic sent economic temperatures declining to well below normal causing tensions between individuals to lessen. Moreover, a sharp decrease in the number of rash adventurers eager for a fight also resulted, and sober settlers faced the bedrock reality of providing food and shelter for themselves and their families. Preserving one's honor became far less important.

The amusements, recreations, sports, and other diversions provided means of escaping from the realities of frontier life. East Texans, along with their fellow citizens throughout the nation, engaged in a variety of such amusements. Newcomers to a community were greeted in many cases by house-raisings, housewarmings, and barn-raisings. Later they would take their turn in providing a similar welcome to other settlers. They took part in rail-splitings, chopping frolics, and quilting bees.

The settlers in a community engaged wholesome "fun" activities with their neighbors. Almost as soon as a few houses were raised, logrollings, barbecues, and dances were held, especially on holidays and election days. In spite of a few amusements that involved women, the major portion of them were vigorous and masculine. Fishing and hunting, including co-operative bear hunts and wolf chasings, were engaged in both for sport and for food for the table.

EARLY EAST TEXAS

The same characteristics that attracted immigrants to Texas and enabled them to survive there, led them to seek diversions eagerly. Dancing and horse racing were among the most common. Dances often lasted all night and even for days at a time. Even though the social mores of the time prohibited the appearance of women on the stage, the men in small Texas villages organized dramatic clubs and played the female parts themselves.

The more hearty among the males with their healthy and humorous outlook on life found an emotional escape in enormous numbers of practical jokes. This form of amusement was epidemic in all frontier communities but in Texas it may have reached its zenith.

Humorous, sentimental, and camp-meeting songs were sung in group singing. The young people from all over the community often found in them an adequate substitute for dancing when a musician was not available. Carousing males often chorused sentimental and ribald tunes in the many saloons found throughout the region. Carousing was especially common on holidays such as the anniversary of the Battle of San Jacinto, Texas independence day, Fourth of July, and Christmas.

On patriotic holidays there were usually parades by military organizations, public reading of patriotic documents, and singing by children in

EARLY EAST TEXAS

addition to dances and barbecues. These were frequently accompanied by dinners usually beginning in the middle of the afternoon where toasts were the order of the day. In some communities fireworks displays and cannon salutes were also holiday festivities.

Instead of the decoration of trees and exchange of presents at Christmas, frontier Texans celebrated the holiday by gatherings of friends and neighbors in small groups beginning on Christmas Eve and extending through Christmas Day itself. Often a whisky punch was prepared and consumed, after which Anglos and Blacks held separate dances.

Frontier style dances were held on every possible occasion, the scarcity of women serving as a fuel for this frontier passion. A single violinist commonly provided the music. Fandangos were also common where, as in Nacogdoches, there was a concentration of Mexican citizens, and some variations of Spanish dances were adopted by Anglo Americans as well. Weddings and christening provided an opportunity for especially large dances with as many as 200 people traveling the horrible roads to attend the ceremony, supper, and dance.

Professional dramatic productions were restricted to the larger towns, and it was not until after annexation that professional drama was revived in Houston and other cities. Their bills of fare were an incongruous mixture of established classics, low comedy, and occasional animal acts. East Texans were not totally dependent upon outsiders for their theatrical entertainment. For example, San Augustine residents developed and supported an enthusiastic Thespian Society organized in 1838 that featured a number of prominent local men who played heroes as well as ladies in sorrowful moods. Negro minstrel shows and "strong men" were also popular in the 1840s as well as the traveling circus.

Gambling fever was a chronic social ailment. Any given individual encountered in Republican Texas likely speculated in land and town sites as a common form of legal gambling. Nacogdoches in pre-Revolutionary days had been known as a "gamblers haven" where every immigrant was considered fair game for trimming. Billiards, bowling alleys, and cockfights promoted wagering in some locales. In 1839, a prominent Texas judge and law teacher called gambling the all too prevalent vice of the day. Men could take risks at roulette, poker, lotteries, and horse racing. The latter was a universal sport in this time period.

As early as 1834 there were several race tracks in the settled portions of East Texas. Most small towns, including the few that were predominantly Spanish in composition, had race courses. Both Nacogdoches and San Augustine among East Texas

EARLY EAST TEXAS

towns had race tracks. Enthusiasm for horse racing persisted throughout the period of the Republic.

Architecture and Daily Life

The houses and other structures of early Texas settlers, marked by their lack of pretense but projecting an air of boldness and expansiveness were reflections of the characters of the men who built and lived in them. Fundamentally, early Texas architecture was plain, rough, strong, angular, and open built more for utility rather than ornament. Their houses were often expressions of their environment built on elevated ground and in proximity to water. Distance from the nearest town fostered simplicity and construction dictated by materials close at hand.

Most of the houses were one- or two-room log cabins known as "dog trot" houses in East Texas with lean-tos adding space when required. They often featured a long porch or porches and an open central hall designed to catch the breezes that help temper the scorching Texas heat. Walls were constructed of roughly hewn logs laid horizontally over each other, fitting together in grooves near or at the ends; spaces between the logs were filled with clay mixed with grass, moss, or sticks. Hand-riven oak "shakes" or boards of the roofs were held in place with stones and weighted poles laid perpendicularly across the shakes and above wooden pegs that extended twelve or eighteen inches beyond the walls to afford protection from rain. Floors were dirt or clay or puncheons--split logs--with roughly dressed flat sides up. Windows were covered with a kind of clarified animal skin. Wide, deep chimneys of sticks and clay with broad hearths of smooth rocks were common.

Regional variations resulted from regional variations in available materials and cultural backgrounds. In Nacogdoches, for example, Spanish architecture dominated the structures built in the formative years. The majority of dwellings were jacales formed by driving pickets or stakes into the ground and fastening them on top by a plate which supported a simple gabled shingle roof. Spaces between the pickets were plastered with the local red clay and then roof lines extended to protect against the rain. Often these plastered walls were covered with an outer layer or stone of adobe.

Some stone buildings were erected in early Nacogdoches but they were rare. Since there was little or no surface stone, rock had to be quarried along the banks of La Nana and Banita Creeks and hauled to the building site. The Stone House (Old Stone Fort) built by Gil Y'Barbo was a simple two-story building with a two-story porch covered by a transverse gabled roof.

After the Mexican Revolution architectural patterns in Nacogdoches gradually came to resemble

EARLY EAST TEXAS

those that had evolved in the American South modified by local conditions. In time, some of the more affluent residents built framed houses with mitered timber frames and flushing and walls with clapboards. Almost from its inception the town of San Augustine, on the other hand, had followed the southern pattern. Although there were a number of hovels as elsewhere in East Texas, many San Augustine homes had colonial fronts, quaint gables and galleries, some full of curious nooks and recesses.

Early houses in Sabine and Shelby Counties were overwhelmingly "dog trot" log cabins with dirt floors and mud packed into the cracks between the logs, no indoor plumbing, and no indoor water supply. Their rooms opened individually off either side of the open central hallway. Crape myrtle and cape jasmine were frequently planted around the house because they provided some shade and were believed to keep insects away.

Wall pegs and shelves were the primitive equivalent of closets in these early log structures. Usually a low shelf near the door supported a water pail with a long-handled gourd hanging nearby. Clothing, rifles, maybe strings of beef or venison, furs, and a mirror hung on pegs elsewhere. Homemade tables, stool, benches and chairs with rawhide bottoms, spinning wheels, and looms were also present in most cabins. One leg beds placed in corners were constructed of rails running from one leg to the walls with hemp ropes or rawhide stretching from rail to rail to support a homemade mattress.

In East Texas, San Augustine dwellings, where the Greek Revival influence was discernible, were among the most beautiful in the nation. They were marked by simplicity in general outline with neoclassical details. J. Pinckney Henderson's two-and-one-half stored residence, modeled after a Virginia mansion, had upper and lower galleries supported by large columns. That of Colonel Stephen W. Blount was one-storied with small, finely proportioned Doric columns. These and other Greek Revival houses gave the town an architectural kinship with the plantation South.

Fire was quite understandably a serious threat in the wood-built structures in East Texas. In the towns an uncontrolled fire could, and did, bring disaster when it destroyed large numbers of structures. For example, a great uncontrolled fire in Nacogdoches in the mid 1850s wiped out the west side of the public square from north to south corners. Towns were forced to rely on "bucket brigades" composed of townspeople armed with buckets and ladders to combat any blaze that erupted within the town limits.

Earlier, in 1845, a fire beginning in a San Augustine store destroyed several downtown buildings before it was checked by tearing down a

EARLY EAST TEXAS

building in it path. A local hotel was saved by the expedient of citizen exertions. They covered the roof with carpets and blankets and kept the front deluged with water thrown from windows.

Maintenance and improvement of streets and bridges was a major consideration for East Texas towns. In rainy seasons mud frequently made streets almost impassable. In the downtown business section, the Nacogdoches streets were often so deep in mud as to stop wagons for several days. The crossings at street corners were often impassable for lady pedestrians. The city, in desperation, often had saw dust, brick bats, and other fill material hauled to downtown crossings.

Food supplies, of course, were essential, causing newly arrived settlers to hasten to plant patches of corn; because they already knew or soon learned that raising a crop of corn was a matter of life or death. Corn was a grain distinctly adapted to fill the role of providing a basic food resource for the consumption of people and their livestock. It was not only comparatively easy to grow and harvest but also simple to prepare for eating.

Before the corn crop was harvested and when the supply of corn was exhausted, venison and the meat of other wild animals became the staple food sources. Dishes prepared from deer, wild turkey, or bear meat were common; while on occasion the flesh

EARLY EAST TEXAS

of wild ducks, geese, "prairie hens." and buffalo steaks and tongue appeared on the table. Milk and butter, however, were rare items.

The basic fare of most Texans was made up of bread made with corn meal, fried beef or venison, and black coffee. Gradually sweet potatoes and bacon were added to the basic diet. Pork was incorporated because hogs could be raised in the woods in great abundance. Somewhat later their fare was expanded to include a few fruits, melons, vegetables, and wild nuts. Pumpkins, sweet potatoes, cabbages, turnips, and peas were early garden crops, while pecan trees flourished in East Texas, particularly in the river bottoms.

Flour was regarded as a luxury item made expensive by the cost of transportation. The proximity of groups of European and Mexican settlers helped introduce some variety into the Texan's diet. In Nacogdoches the Mexicans made thin, flat, unleavened tortillas from corn meal, which Anglos soon learned to like. Eggs prepared in various unusual ways and a stew made of beef, chicken, or other kind of meat with pumpkin and a large quantity of red pepper were also favorite Mexican dishes. Mexican tamales made of corn-meal, chopped meat, and Cayenne pepper wrapped in corn husk and boiled also became popular.

Texas coffee, usually drunk without sugar or

cream, was notoriously potent. Although the earliest Anglo settlers could not afford to purchase coffee, the coffee can or coffee pot became standard equipment for home or while traveling.

From 1821 to the eve of statehood, life in Nacogdoches and elsewhere in East Texas resembled that of many frontier southern communities. The principle staples of diet were corn, and a wide variety of meats (beef, cabrito, pork, mutton, venison, bear, raccoon, squirrel, turkey, and duck). Fresh vegetables including peas, squash, beans, pumpkins, and potatoes were grown in garden patches. Wild peaches, blackberries, persimmons, pomegranates, and melons grew in the forests surrounding the town as did walnuts, hickory nuts, and pecans.

Among males, tobacco was almost as indispensable as coffee. They chewed an inordinant quantity of the weed. Cigars were more commonly smoked than cigarettes. East Texans soon launched into the production of tobacco, and a cigar factory was established in Nacogdoches. Older Anglo American women were often pipe smokers, while many of the younger females used ("dipped") snuff.

The rugged individualists that settled in Texas during the days of the Republic drank enormous quantities of intoxicants. Saloons and "grog shops" were among the first business establishments to appear in frontier towns. The most common drinks were whiskey, brandy, and cognac with gin and wines also consumed. Mixed drinks, notably a whiskey punch, were popular in Texas hotels. Holidays, election days, and political campaign speaking were time of unrestrained license in alcohol consumption.

Clothing for Texas residents, especially those living on the frontier, often presented serious problem. Dress ranged from the reliable roughness of buckskin to the refined elegance of broadcloth. In 1830, a visitor to Nacogdoches commented that apparel extended from virtual nudity to genteel costume. Because the area was peopled by a variety of ethnic groups and social classes, their dress reflected the tastes and styles of Indians, Frenchmen, and Anglo Americans. For most residents dress was of the plainest sort with buckskin and homespun linen shirts a common sight.

Buckskin gradually gave way to homespun cotton materials. Clothes of whatever type were almost invariably made by womenfolk who carded, spun, and wove both cotton and wool cloth. Women commonly wore dresses made from homespun cotton, and bonnets, while the men sported coats and pants of homespun cotton or wool and hats made of palmetto or straw. Blankets were formed into overcoats, while they also wore their blankets poncho style.

As families became more affluent and mercantile stores more accessible, some women were

EARLY EAST TEXAS

able to secure ready-to-wear clothes or fabrics purchased by the yard. When they could afford them, shoes, calico materials, silk crepes and ginghams were also purchased from local merchants.

Getting from place to place amid the forests and waterways posed another troublesome problem for early settlers in East Texas. The first immigrants to enter from the east traveled over traces that were little more than Indian trails on foot or on horseback with their belongings and goods on pack horses or pack mules. Stagecoach lines did not begin operations in East Texas until after annexation to the United States. In the 1850s several stage lines had their headquarters in Nacogdoches. One of them traveled the general route of the San Antonio Road, a second ran eastward into Louisiana, and a third traveled between Washington-on-the-Brazos and Nacogdoches.

Movement of persons and freight was severly hampered by the absence of decent roadways. The Camino Real between Nacogdoches and San Antonio, for example, had been in constant use since early in the Eighteenth Century, but as late as 1846 in some places it was only a mass of wagon ruts that cut through the forest or over the prairie. Lesser roads were little more than cow or deer trails, easy to distinguish but terrible to traverse.

Difficulty of overland travel was compounded

EARLY EAST TEXAS

by the problem of crossing rivers and other waterways especially in the eastern section of the nation. East-west travel was most troublesome as the rivers and other streams tended to flow in a north-south direction necessitating numerous water crossings. As time passed ferries were gradually installed at strategic points on authorization by a county government.

As a consequence, most travel over the primitive roads was by horseback. Goods were hauled in giant wagons drawn by mules or oxen. In good weather goods were transported relatively easily but very slowly. In wet weather, the roads turned into quagmires, and freight did not move at all.

Ox-wagons carried freight from Natchitoches, Louisiana to San Augustine in East Texas. Such wagons drawn by three yoke of oxen could transport some 3,000 pounds of goods. Far from a major Gulf port, the residents of East Texas hauled their cotton and other produce to market by wagon. Most of this freight went from points west of the Sabine River to Shreveport where it could be loaded on rivercraft and shipped downriver to New Orleans.

In 1839, the Congress of the Republic directed that counties along the route should construct a road from Washington-on-the-Brazos to Jasper in East Texas and from there to the Sabine River. The finances of the Republic were such, however, that the nation could offer little in the way of assistance, most roads were little more than trails from which the trees and brush had been cleared.

The uncertainty of travel in the days of the Republic meant that no effective postal system functioned. A few post offices and mail routes connecting the principal towns were established before the Revolution, but service was hampered by inadequate roads, high water, official mismanagement, and robberies. The business of carrying the mail was neither lucrative nor peaceful. Private firms that contracted with the government to transport the mail often had difficulty being compensated or found that inflation had made the contract virtually worthless.

The untrustworthiness of the government mail service prompted resort to private carriers. When the government postal service broke down almost completely in 1842, groups of citizens in Nacogdoches and elsewhere contributed to private subscriptions with which to pay mail carriers. Not until well after annexation was a reasonably effective mail service established.

The numerous rivers and streams of East Texas offered an alternative to overland travel for people and freight. But in practice the long, meandering rivers were difficult even for shallow-draft steamers and other craft to negotiate. Most overflowed during the spring rains, all needed clearing, and some were chocked by masses of driftwood called "rafts."

Nevertheless, by 1839 steamboats were making regular trips up and down the Sabine River from November to the end of June, and the following year a steamboat departed from Sabine Pass, and after days of battling with all the impediments to navigation on the Sabine River of the time, reached Fullerton's Landing just south of Sabinetown in Sabine County. At least two other steamers made trips upriver by 1842 where they were loaded with cotton for the return trip.

The Shelby County community named East Hamilton was founded after the Sabine River was opened to steamboat traffic in 1837. It was the first stop in the county for north-bound boats and the last point at which the river widened sufficiently and was deep enough to allow the larger boats to turn around.

During 1841 the Angelina River was cleared through private subscriptions by the citizens of Nacogdoches, and by 1844 a keel boat, the <u>Thomas J. Rusk,</u> made regular trips between Sabine Pass and the Nacogdoches County town of Patonia located about twelve miles south of Nacogdoches. Later, in 1847, a steamboat came up to river to Patonia and by 1849 made trips as regularly as the water level would permit.

The principal freight of these river craft

EARLY EAST TEXAS

downstream was cotton. Upriver, however, they would be loaded with sugar, flour, molasses, salt, iron, nails, castings, domestic cloth, ready-made clothing, shoes, hats, and tin ware. Although many of the farms and settlements in East Texas were on or near rivers, water transportation was largely a disappointment as a travel medium.

    The difficulties of travel over unimproved roads and unbridged waterways were so great that the San Augustine-Nacogdoches district of East Texas was isolated from the Clarksville region of Red River County and the Brazos Valley-Houston area. Improved travel conditions simply awaited the coming of the railroads.

    Since East Texans found travel by land and along the region's waterways troublesome and mail service unreliable, communication with those living in other sections of the country was severly limited. Newspapers attempted to supply some measure of information to their readers, but obtaining news, other than local happenings, was hard to obtain. They too were handicapped by the difficulties produced by poor mail service.

    Perhaps for this reason the newspapers of early Texas were poor sources of news compared with those that began to be published late in the Nineteenth Century. In East Texas, particularly, news from the outside world came generally through New Orleans, up the Red River to Natchitoches, and across the Sabine to San Augustine and Nacogdoches. They did not regularly print articles concerning social activities, and good taste dictated that the names of ladies not be printed except under extraordinary circumstances. On the other hand, they were filled with political news and sharp editorial comment on public affairs of the time. Thus, the people who read them were well informed on important current issues.

Between 1813 and 1846, at least eighty-six different newspapers made their appearance in Texas. Among them were the Gaceta de Texas that published one broadside in Nacogdoches in 1813, the El Mexico one issue in 1813, The Texas Republican a few issues in 1819, the Mexican Advocate some issues in 1829, The Texas Chronicle a year of issues between 1836 and 1845, and the Nacogdoches News three years of issues after 1846. The first Nacogdoches newspaper to be published on a continuing basis, however, did not appear until the decade of the 1890s.

In San Augustine A. W. Canfield began publishing the Journal and Advertiser in 1840, changing its name in 1842 to the Redlander. This newspaper was probably the most influential news source in East Texas for many years thereafter with a wide circulation. Canfield, a New York native, was a man with great taste and style. His editorial ability, keen sense and sound judgment enabled him to produce a paper whose opinions were read and respected throughout Texas. He published important speeches by prominent men, letters and articles on leading questions of the day, State papers, reports of political meetings, and nominations of candidates for public office. The <u>Redlander</u>, under his direction, became a weekly journal of national interest, particularly devoted to the affairs of East Texas and San Augustine.

Texas newspapers frequently printed whole columns copied from American newspapers and magazines dealing with events, industries, and arts in foreign nations including, of course, the United States. They also copied local and foreign news from other Texas newspapers. The columns that received the most attention were those concerned with politics, and most papers aligned themselves with a political faction featuring extremely partisan reporting of much news.

Throughout most, if not all, of the period of the Republic some East Texas communities, notably Nacogdoches and San Augustine, continued to grow and prosper in spite of the devastating Panic of 1837 which crippled the economy of the United States. Nacogdoches seemed destined to retain its ranking as one of the major cities of Texas. Worsening economic conditions in the Republic and in the United States combined with increasing geographic isolation served

EARLY EAST TEXAS

to radically alter that prospect for Nacogdoches and all of East Texas.

EPILOGUE

After almost a decade of procrastination, the United States Congress passed a joint resolution offering annexation as an American state to the Republic of Texas. Popular sentiment favoring annexation had been demonstrated on at least two occasions: a vote in 1836 that was almost unanimous in favor and in the national election of 1844. East Texas heavily populated by settlers from the United States overwhelmingly supported annexation whenever the question arose.

President Anson Jones called for a convention to meet July 4, 1845, and when the Republic's Congress met in June the offer of the United States was unanimously accepted, the President's call for election of delegates to a constitutional convention was approved, and adjournment was also quickly approved. In the July 4th election, Thomas J. Rusk, Joseph L. Hogg, William B. Ochiltree, and Charles S. Taylor were chosen to represent Nacogdoches County; while Nicholas H. Darnell and James P. Henderson represented San Augustine County; James M. Burroughs represented Sabine County; and Archibald W. O. Hicks and Emory Raines represented Shelby

County.[61]

The distribution of delegates reflects the relative political strength of the four geographical regions of the Republic. The eight eastern counties, including Nacogdoches, San Augustine, Sabine, and Shelby, were allotted thirteen delegates, ten of which represented the four named counties; the twelve western counties given fourteen; the eleven middle counties twenty-three; and the five northern counties eleven. A number of those East Texas delegates had held important political positions before being selected: Darnell had been a member of the Tennessee legislature; Henderson had been Attorney General and Secretary of State of the Republic; Rusk had been Secretary of War, Congressman, and Chief Justice of the Republic. In addition, Rusk was easily chosen as the President of the Convention.

The proposed constitution for the new State of Texas drafted by the 1845 Convention was approved along with the annexation referendum by an overwhelming majority vote of Texans October 13, 1845, and by the Congress of the United States in December. President James K. Polk signed the act of annexation almost immediately, and in a brief ceremony February 19, 1846, President Anson Jones

---

[61] See Appendix IV for more information on these delegates.

EARLY EAST TEXAS

formally handed over executive authority to the first Texas Governor, James Pinckney Henderson of San Augustine County. The first Texas state legislature chose Sam Houston and Nacogdoches County resident Thomas J. Rusk as the first United States Senators from Texas. David S. Kaufman of Sabine County became the first Texan elected to the national House of Representatives.

In the first election for members of the Texas state legislature, Isaac Parker of Houston County and Joseph L. Hogg of Nacogdoches County became state senators from District Four composed of Nacogdoches, Rusk and Houston Counties. John Brown, Haden H. Edwards, and David Muckleroy became state representatives representing Nacogdoches County. William B. Ochiltree of Nacogdoches County became the first judge of the Sixth Judicial District and Richard S. Walker also of Nacogdoches County its first District Attorney.

Jesse J. Robinson was the first state senator to represent Sabine, Jasper, and Harrison Counties; while James M. Burroughs and James M. Noble became its first state representatives. Benjamin R. Wallace was the first state senator from San Augustine and Shelby Counties, and William F. Echols and James Truitt its first state representatives. William C. Edwards and Henry W. Sublett were the first state representatives from San Augustine County.

EARLY EAST TEXAS

In the years after annexation the Nacogdoches-San Augustine region entered a new era in its history. While much of Texas experienced boom times in the time between annexation and the eruption of the Civil War in 1861, East Texas did not share in that prosperity. The stringent immigration and trade regulations of Spanish-Mexican times that were instrumental in making San Augustine and Nacogdoches major entry points for persons making their way to Texas were no longer in force. With their disappearance and a variety of other entry points available, these East Texas settlements gradually became isolated "backwater" communities. Moreover, they slowly ceased to be market centers for the region.

The principal cause of the decline was their geographic location. They no longer lay athwart a well-traveled transportation route. The old San Antonio Road, once their main link with areas east and west, had deteriorated into a near impassable quagmire during much of the year. There was no significant waterway as only light draft steamboats could make their way up the Sabine and Angelina Rivers and only navigable for six to nine months in a year. Gulf Coast communities such as Galveston and Houston became the principal trade centers rather than the inland towns.

A contemporary historian lamented that as years passed developments in transportation--

EARLY EAST TEXAS

steamboats, railroads, and ships--routed people and goods around and beyond East Texas and thereby stripped the region of the advantages of its geographic location. As a result, the towns of the region slowly became sleepy backwoods trading centers not unlike thousands of such places throughout the rural South.

An Norwegian immigrant visiting Nacogdoches in 1845 observed that there was no poor relief apparent because the townspeople cared for the poor and needy. She also noted the degree of freedom and equality she found in social relationships and public matters. Obviously, she chose to ignore the differences between free white residents and their submerged black slaves and the more subtle distinctions between Anglos and Hispanics. The fundamental honesty of the residents, the near absence of thievery, and the absence of locks on the doors of houses also caught her attention.

The economy of the East Texas region in the years following annexation was based on the small farmer who owned a few slaves, raised crops to feed his family, and sold whatever cotton he raised for his cash income. Although cotton was easily the major row crop, East Texas farmers also cultivated corn, wheat, and sugar cane. Stock farming was not a major concern, although most farmers owned some livestock, including horses, cattle, sheep, and hogs. The area farmers were not large land owners nor slave owners. Persons of substantial means were rare; in Nacogdoches County, for example, the 1850 Census revealed only eight men who owned real estate valued at $25,000 or more, and only one individual with a substantial number of slaves.

People of the Republic of Mexico were reluctant to agree that they had lost the province of Texas. Internal turmoil and unsettled conditions throughout most of the period from the ratification of the treaty ending the Texas Revolution until late in the decade of the 1840s prevented them from taking concerted action to reassert authority over their former possession. To forestall any overt attempt by the Mexican government, soon after annexation became evident General Zachary Taylor and a strong contingent of American troops were ordered to establish a headquarters at Corpus Christi. Later, when Taylor's sent a portion of his forces south toward the Rio Grande, Mexican troops were dispatched to intercept the Americans.

The Mexican position was that under no circumstances did the southern boundary of Texas extend beyond the Nueces River to the Rio Grande. Skirmishes between Americans and Mexicans occurred in April and May of 1846 and later battles were fought at Palo Alto and Resaca de la Palma near Brownsville. Whereupon the Congress of the United States declared war, and General Taylor began driving

EARLY EAST TEXAS

the Mexican troops toward Monterrey. Taylor asked Governor Henderson of Texas for two regiments of infantry and two of cavalry. Henderson responded promptly and was granted a leave of absence to take command of the Texas forces who might be mustered into the service of the United States.

Before the war ended a total of 8,018 Texans enlisted. At least two companies of East Texans volunteered for service. A company of Nacogdoches County men commanded by Captain James R. Arnold joined Taylor's army while it was camped at Corpus Christi. Before war's end they had participated in two major battles: Monterrey and Buena Vista. A second company captained by David Muckleroy of Nacogdoches was recruited in East Texas and mustered in at San Antonio.

The war ended in 1848 with the Treaty of Guadalupe Hidalgo. By its terms, Mexico, for the first time, renounced all claims to Texas and accepted the Rio Grande as the southern boundary between the United States and the Republic of Mexico.

In spite of a depressed economy, threat of invasion by Mexican military forces, and other factors that might have discouraged immigration, numbers of individuals and families coming to East Texas grew from 1836 to 1860. At least 388 families arrived in Nacogdoches County alone. The majority of these immigrants came from the states of the Old South.

EARLY EAST TEXAS

Some seventy percent were from Alabama, Tennessee, and Mississippi. Most of the remainder were from Louisiana, Georgia, Arkansas, Kentucky, and Missouri. A consequence of this wave of immigrants was to strengthen its ties to the American South and its slave-holding tradition.

Handicapped by the lack of effective land transportation, staggered by the effects of the Civil War, and struggling to recover from the aftermath of Radical Reconstruction, East Texas as late as 1875 had not regained the place of prominence and influence it held under Spain, Mexico, or the Republic of Texas. Contending with the problem not only of rebuilding its prewar economy, but also of establishing a diversified economic foundation for life for the first time, it would be many years before it regained some semblance of its pre-war status. Meanwhile the towns and rural communities of East Texas slumbered until the decade of the 1880s awaiting the coming of railroads.

EARLY EAST TEXAS

APPENDICES

APPENDICES

APPENDIX I

EAST TEXAS CONGRESSMEN: REPUBLIC OF TEXAS
    First Congress (1836-1837)

[Legend: NAME; age; place of previous residence; experience; occupation]

SENATE:
    San Augustine District
HENRY W. AUGUSTINE; 41; Alabama; Consultation of 1835
SHELBY CORZINE; 43; lawyer
    Nacogdoches District
ROBERT A. IRION; 30; Mississippi; physician
    Shelby and Sabine District
WILLIS H. LANDRUM; 31; Tennessee; Shelby County Board of Land Commissioners; farmer-merchant

HOUSE OF REPRESENTATIVES:
    Nacogdoches County District
JOHN K. ALLEN; 26; New York; land speculator-town promoter
HAYDEN S. ARNOLD; 31; Tennessee; farmer
HADEN H. EDWARDS; 24; Louisiana; stockman

EARLY EAST TEXAS

San Augustine County District
JOSEPH ROWE; 34; North Carolina; judge; physician
WILLIAM W. HOLMAN; 30; Tennesse; farmer
Sabine County District
JOHN BOYD; 40; Tennessee; farmer
Shelby County District
SYDNEY O. PENNINGTON; 27; Arkansas; Convention of 1836; scientific research

SECOND CONGRESS (1837-1838)

SENATE:
San Augustine District
HENRY W. AUGUSTINE (See First Congress)
JOHN A. GREER; 35; Kentucky; farmer
Nacogdoches District
ISAAC W. BURTON; 32; Georgia; Indian Commissioner; lawyer
Shelby and Sabine District
EMORY RAINES; 37; Tennessee; farmer
HOUSE OF REPRESENTATIVES:
Sabine County
JOHN BOYD (See First Congress)
WILLIAM CLARK, JR.; 49; Louisiana; Convention of 1836; Sabine County Board of Land Commissioners; merchant-farmer
Nacogdoches District

EARLY EAST TEXAS

KELSEY H. DOUGLASS; merchant
THOMAS J. RUSK; 44; South Carolina; Consultation of 1835, Convention of 1836, Secretary of War; lawyer
    Shelby County District
JOHN ENGLISH; 54; Tennessee; Convention of 1833; farmer
WILLIAM PIERPONT; merchant-farmer
    San Augustine District
JOSEPH ROWE (See First Congress); Speaker of the House
CHARLTON THOMPSON; lawyer

THIRD CONGRESS (1838-1839)

SENATE:
    Nacogdoches-Houston County District
ISAAC W. BURTON (See Second Congress)
JOHN A. GREER (See Second Congress)
    Shelby-Sabine County District
EMORY RAINS (See Second Congress)

HOUSE OF REPRESENTATIVES:
    San Augustine County District
ISAAC CAMPBELL; 36
EZEKIEL CULLEN; 24; Georgia; lawyer
    Shelby County District
JOHN M. HANSFORD; Kentucky; lawyer; Speaker

EARLY EAST TEXAS

of the House
ALVEY R. JOHNSON; farmer(?)
    Nacogdoches County District
DAVID S. KAUFMAN; 25; Louisiana; lawyer
KINDRED H. MUSE; 37; Registrar, Nacogdoches Land Office; farmer
    Sabine County District
JOHN PAYNE; Justice of the Peace; farmer(?)

FOURTH CONGRESS (1839-1840)

SENATE:
    Nacogdoches-Houston County District
ISAAC W. BURTON (See Second Congress)
    Shelby-Sabine-Harrison County District
JAMES T. GAINES; 63; Louisiana(?); Alcalde, Sheriff, Convention of 1836; merchant-ferryman
    San Augustine County District
JOHN A. GREER (See Second Congress)

HOUSE OF REPRESENTATIVES:
    Sabine County District
SAMUEL L. BENTON; c.55; Missouri; farmer
    San Augustine County District

EARLY EAST TEXAS

SAMUEL S. DAVIS; farmer(?)
SAMUEL (SAM) HOUSTON; 46; Arkansas; Tennessee District Attorney, U. S. Congressman, and Governor, President, Republic of Texas; lawyer
    Shelby County District
JOHN M. HANDSFORD (See Third Congress)
MOSES F. ROBERTS; 36; Tennessee; farmer(?)
    Nacogdoches County District
DAVID S. KAUFMAN (See Third Congress); Speaker of the House
KINDRED H. MUSE (See Third Congress)

FIFTH CONGRESS (1840-1841)

SENATE:
    Shelby-Sabine-Harrison County District
JAMES T. GAINES (See Fourth Congress)
    San Augustine County District
JOHN A. GREER (See Second Congress)
    Nacogdoches-Houston County District
KINDRED H. MUSE (See Fourth Congress)

HOUSE OF REPRESENTATIVES:
    San Augustine County District
HENRY W. AUGUSTINE (See First Congress)
SAMUEL (SAM) HOUSTON (See Fourth Congress)
    Sabine County District

EARLY EAST TEXAS

S. SLADE BARNETT; farmer
    Shelby County District
JOHN S. BELL; farmer
MOSES F. ROBERTS (See Fourth Congress)
    Nacogdoches County District
DAVID S. KAUFMAN (See Third Congress); Speaker of the House
JAMES S. MAYFIELD; 31; Tennessee; lawyer

SIXTH CONGRESS (1841-1842)

SENATE:
    Shelby-Sabine-Harrison District
JAMES T. GAINES (See Fourth Congress)
LEWONARD RANDAL; 41; North Carolina; physician
    San Augustine District
JOHN A. GREER (See Second Congress)
    Nacogdoches-Houston District
KINDRED H. MUSE (See Third Congress)

HOUSE OF REPRESENTATIVES:
    San Augustine District
KENNETH L. ANDERSON; 36; Tennessee; Collector of Customs, District Attorney; lawyer, Speaker of the House
NICHOLAS H. DARNELL; 34; Tennessee; Tennessee Legislature; soldier

EARLY EAST TEXAS

Nacogdoches County District
JOHN BROWN; 54; South Carolina; lawyer-farmer
JAMES S. MAYFIELD (See Fifth Congress)
Shelby County District
WILLIAM H. HEWITT; 47; Georgia; farmer
MOSES F. ROBERTS (See Fourth Congress)
Sabine County District
WILLIS H. LANDRUM (See First Congress)

SEVENTH CONGRESS (1842-1843)

SENATE:
San Augustine District
JOHN A. GREER (See Second Congress); President pro tem
Nacogdoches-Houston District
KINDRED H. MUSE (See Third Congress)
Shelby-Sabine-Harrison District
LEONARD RANDAL (See Sixth Congress)

HOUSE OF REPRESENTATIVES:
Shelby County District
JOHN DIAL; farmer
WILLIAM H. HEWITT (See Sixth Congress)
San Augustine District
NICHOLAS H. DARNELL (See Sixth Congress); Speaker of the House
RICHARDSON A. SCURRY; 30; Tennessee; District

EARLY EAST TEXAS

Attorney; lawyer
    Sabine County District
JESSE J. ROBINSON; 45; North Carolina; farmer
    Nacogdoches County District
WILLIAM F. SPARKS; 28; Mississippi; farmer
JESSE WALLING; 48; Tennessee; farmer-cotton ginner

EIGHTH CONGRESS (1843-1844)

SENATE:
    San Augustine District
JOHN A. GREER (See Second Congress); President pro tem
    Shelby-Sabine-Harrison District
DAVID S. KAUFMAN (See Third Congress)
    Nacogdoches-Houston-Rusk District
ISAAC PARKER; 50; Illinois; farmer

HOUSE OF REPRESENTATIVES:
    San Augustine District
NICHOLAS H. DARNELL (See Seventh Congress)
RICHARDSON A. SCURRY (See Seventh Congress); Speaker of the House
    Nacogdoches District
JOSEPH L. HOGG; 36; Alabama; lawyer
    Sabine District
WILLIAM MEANS; Georgia; Sheriff, tax collector;

EARLY EAST TEXAS

farmer(?)
> Shelby District

JAMES TRUITT; 48; North Carolina; farmer(?)

NINTH CONGRESS (1845)

SENATE:
> San Augustine District

JOHN A. GREER (See Second Congress); President pro tem
> Sabine-Shelby-Harrison District

DAVID S. KAUFMAN (See Third Congress)
> Nacogdoches-Houston-Rusk District

ISAAC PARKER (See Eighth Congress)

HOUSE OF REPRESENTATIVES:
> San Augustine District

JOHN S. FORD; 30; Tennessee; physician
BENJAMIN R. WALLACE; 45; Virginia; lawyer
> Shelby District

MIDDLETON T. JOHNSON; 35; Alabama; Alabama Legislature; lawyer-judge
> Sabine District

WILLIAM MEANS (See Eighth Congress)
> Nacogdoches District

JOHN H. MOFFITT; teacher

[Sources: Biographical Directory of the Texan

EARLY EAST TEXAS

Conventions and Congresses and Gateway to Texas, Vol. I.

APPENDIX II

DISTRICT AND COUNTY JUDGES: REPUBLIC OF TEXAS

FIRST JUDICIAL DISTRICT
Shelby Corzine (San Augustine County)
Ezekiel W. Cullen (San Augustine County)
Anthony B. Shelby (Galveston County)
Thomas Johnson (San Augustine County)
Richard Morris (Harris & Galveston Counties)
John B. Jones (Galveston)

FIFTH JUDICIAL DISTRICT
Edward T. Branch (Liberty County)
George W. Terrell (San Augustine County)
William B. Ochiltree (Nacogdoches and San Augustine Counties)
Royal T. Wheeler (Nacogdoches and San Augustine Counties)

SIXTH JUDICIAL DISTRICT
Richardson A. Scurry (San Augustine County)
Patrick C. Jack (Galveston County)
Milford P. Norton (Galveston County)

NACOGDOCHES COUNTY CHIEF JUSTICES

EARLY EAST TEXAS

Charles S. Taylor
William W. Winfield
William Hart(e)

SABINE COUNTY CHIEF JUSTICES
Matthew A. Parker
William P. Wyche
Robert Gallantly
Francis T. Gaines
Richard R. Jowel

SAN AUGUSTINE COUNTY CHIEF JUSTICES
William McFarland
Edwin O. LaGrand
Alexander M. Davis
Robert H. Foote
John C. Brooke
Alfred Polk

SHELBY COUNTY CHIEF JUSTICES
George W. Lusk
Archibald W. O. Hicks
James Mason
Albert T. Jones

[Source: Judges of the Republic of Texas]

APPENDIX III

EAST TEXAS BAR (1850)

Nacogdoches County
Thomas J. Rusk
William B. Ochiltree
Richard Sheckle Walker
Charles Stanfield Taylor
Amos Clark

W. C. Pollock
Thomas J. Jennings
R. R. Page
Ashbel Green
William C. Duffield

Sabine County
David S. Kaufman
Jesse J. Robinson

Frederick W. Fontleroy
Benjamin G. Burks

Shelby County
Archibald W. O. Hicks
W. R. Owens
Levy H. Ashcroft

Daniel M. Short
Richard Hooper
William A. Holland

San Augustine County
James P. Henderson
Oran M. Roberts
Henry W. Sublett
H. M. Kinsey
J. F. Childers(?)
Alexander H. Evans

James Davenport
B. J. Lewis
Franklin B. Sublett
Franklin B. Sexton
Malcolm G. Anderson
Charlton Payne

EARLY EAST TEXAS

Jesse Benton   William G. Anderson
Benjamin R. Wallace   James Ardrey

[Source: 1850 U. S. Census]

APPENDIX IV

EAST TEXAS DELEGATES; CONVENTION OF 1845

JAMES M. BURROUGHS (Sabine County)
NICHOLAS H. DARNELL (San Augustine County)
JAMES P. HENDERSON (San Augustine County)
ARCHIBALD W. O. HICKS (Shelby County)
EMORY RAINS (Shelby County)
JOSEPH L. HOGG (Nacogdoches County)
WILLIAM B. OCHILTREE (Nacogdoches County)
THOMAS J. RUSK (Nacogdoches County) President of the Convention

[Source: <u>Biographical Directory of the Texan Conventions and Congresses</u>]

APPENDIX V

EAST TEXAS PHYSICIANS (1850)

Nacogdoches County
James H. Starr
Robert Anderson Irion
George Strother Hyde
Samuel Stivers
Thomas Jefferson Johnson
S. W. Kirk

Osborn. H. Boykin
John D. Windam
James Henry Sharp
Joseph P. Sharp
A. F. Strode
Elijah Allen

San Augustine County
Benjamin Franklin Sharp
William A. Sharp
Leonard Randal
Charles J. Smith
John C. Womack

Joseph Wood
Isaiah Jackson Roberts
Oscar Fitzallen
J. J. Sims
Nathan P. West

Sabine County
Robert K. Goodloe
James Low
Lawrence McGuire
Creed T. McDaniel

John R. Smith
Lycurgus Edward Griffith
Robert J. Oliphant
Richard Meador

Shelby County
John S. Pursely

T. G. Williams

EARLY EAST TEXAS

Jackson Grady William P. Landrum
E. C. Mauldin James H. Stuart
Fresuius Amote
_____

[Source: 1850 U. S. Census]

EARLY EAST TEXAS

EARLY EAST TEXAS

BIBLIOGRAPHY

General Sources

Blake, Robert B., Research Collection and Supplement. Ninety-three volumes of transcripts and translations of materials pertaining to the history of East Texas and Nacogdoches County. East Texas Research Center, R. W. Steen Library, Stephen F. Austin State University, Nacogdoches, Texas.

Crocket, George L., Two Centuries in East Texas: A History of San Augustine County and Surrounding Territory from 1685 (Austin: Hart Graphics), Reprint ed., 1982.

Ericson, Carolyn R., Nacogdoches: Gateway to Texas: A Biographical Directory, 1773-1849 (Nacogdoches: Ericson Books) Vol. I, Revised ed., 1991.

Fehrenbach, T. R., Lone Star: A History of Texas and the Texans, (New York: Collier Books), 1980.

Foote, Henry C., Texas and the Texans (Philadelphia: Thomas, Cowpertwait, & Co.), Reprint Ed., 1935.

Hogan, William Ranson, The Texas Republic: A Social and Economic History (Austin: The University of Texas Press), 1946.

EARLY EAST TEXAS

Richardson, Rupert N., Texas: The Lone Star State (New York: Prentice-Hall, Inc.), 1943.
Tyler, Ron, ed., The New Handbook of Texas (Austin: The Texas State Historical Association), 6 vols., 1996.

Topical Sources

Biographical Directory of the Texan Conventions and Congresses:1832-1845 (Austin:Book Exchange), 1941.
Brackenridge, R. Douglas, Voice in the Wilderness: A History of the Cumberland Presbyterian Church in Texas (San Antonio: Trinity University Press), 1968.
Clark, Mary W., Chief Bowles and the Texas Cherokees (Norman: University of Oklahoma Press), 1971.
Centennial Story of Texas Baptists (Dallas: Baptist General Convention of Texas), 1936.
Ericson, Joe E., Judges of the Republic of Texas (Dallas: Taylor Publishing Co.), 1980.
Personalities on the East Texas Frontier: Brief Narratives of Their Lives and Times (Nacogdoches: Ericson Books), 1998.
The Nacogdoches Story: An Informal History (Bowie, Md.: Heritage Books), 2000.
Horton, Alexander, A. Horton: Patriot of the republic

of Texas (San Augustine: Malone Printing), 1984.

James Frederick Gomer Chapter, Daughters of the Republic of Texas, History and Tax Records of the Sabine District and Sabine County, Texas (Hemphill: privately published) n. d.

McCoy, Patricia R., Shelby County Sampler (Lufkin: Lufkin Printing Co.), 1982.

McDaniel, Robert C., Sabine County, Texas: The First One Hundred and Fifty Years (1836-1986) (Waco: Texian Press), 1987.

McDonald, Archie P., ed., Nacogdoches: Wilderness Outpost to Modern City (Burnett: Eakin Press), 1980.

Middleton, John W., History of the Regulators and Moderators and the Shelby County War in 1841 and 1842 (Fort Worth: Loving Publishing Co.), 1883.

Partin, James G., Carolyn R. Ericson, Joe E. Ericson, and Archie P. McDonald, Nacogdoches (Lufkin: Best of Texas Publishers), 1995.

Phelan, Macum, A History of Early Methodism in Texas (1817-1866) (Nashville: Cokesbury Press), 1946.

Red, George P., The Medicine Man in Texas (Houston: Standard Printing Co.), 1930.

Red, William S., A History of the Presbyterian Church in Texas (Austin: The Steck Co.),

EARLY EAST TEXAS

1936.

Shelby County Historical Commission, <u>History of Shelby County, Texas: 1988</u> (Dallas: Curtis Media Corp.), 1988.

Smith, Jesse G., <u>Heroes of the Saddle Bags: A History of Christian Denominations in the Republic of Texas</u> (San Antonio: The Naylor Company), 1951.

White, Edna M. and Blanche Toole, <u>Sabine County Historical Sketches and Genealogical Records</u> (Beaumont: LaBelle Printing Co.), 1972.

INDEX

-A-

Aguayo
  Marquez San Miguel de, 15
Alabama, 86, 93, 211, 279, 206
  Blount County, 210
  Tuscumbia, 201
  Watauga County, 135
Alamo, 249
Alarcon
  Don Martin de, 14
Alazan River, 54
Alcalde, 78
Alexander
  Robert, 200
Alford
  Needham J., 198, 204
Alto, 118
Anahuac, 110, 123, 125
Andalusia, 21
Anderson
  Bailey, 99, 111
  Kenneth L., 224
Angelina River, 3, 13, 94, 96, 113, 155, 156, 176(2), 267, 275
Archer
  Branch T., 136, 137
Arkansas, 279
Arkansas Post, 67
Arkansas Territory, 141, 160, 197
Arnold
  James R., 278
Arroyo Hondo, 14, 15, 35
Atascosito, 61
Attoyac River, 4, 45, 50, 59, 89, 91, 95, 99, 136, 176, 200
Augustine
  Henry W., 135, 156, 180, 183
Austin, 248
  John, 62
  Stephen F., 62, 76, 78, 81, 86, 128, 132, 133, 137, 139, 219
Ayish Bayou, 56, 65, 88, 92, 96, 99, 104, 129, 167
Ayish Bayou District, 3, 89, 93, 96, 99, 127, 128, 136, 195
Ayish Bayou settlement, 131

-B-

Bacon
  Samuel, 206
  Sumner, 180, 198, 204
Bancroft
  H. H., 71
Banita Creek, 7, 14, 20, 26, 65, 100, 257

Baptist Church, 196, 207, 212
Barr
  William, 4, 33, 68
Barr and Davenport, 33
Bastrop
  Baron Felipe Enrique Neri de, 77
Battle of Nacogdoches, 109, 114, 121, 122, 135, 144, 154
Battle of New Orleans, 44, 58
Battle of Rosillo, 53
Battle of Salado, 157
Battle of San Jacinto, 136, 140, 144, 148, 149, 191, 204, 242, 253
Battle of the Neches, 161
Battle of Velasco, 138
Bays
  Joseph E., 207
Beall
  Charles, 77
  Tabitha (Beall), 77
Bean
  Peter Ellis, 44
Beauchamp
  Thomas D., 128
Berry
  John O., 183
  Radford, 226
Bethel Baptist Church, 208
Bevil, 111
Bevil (Jasper), 226
Bidais Creek, 25, 135
Big Thicket, 93
Billingsley
  Council, 210
Blackburn
  Ephriam, 44
Blair
  Joshua, 56
Blake
  Bennett, 186
Blanco
  Governor Victor, 86
Blount
  Stephen W., 236, 259
Board of Commissioners, 229
Board of Land Commissioners, 163(2), 170
  Nacogdoches County, 243
Bolivar Point, 60, 62
Bonaparte
  Napoleon, 37
Bonnell
  G. W., 159
Border Baptist Church, 209
Borreagas Creek, 118

306

INDEX

Borreagas Crossing, 118
Bowie
  Jim, 114
Bowles
  Chief (The Bowl), 72, 160
Bradburn
  John Davis, 123, 125
Bradley
  John M., 128, 165, 167
Bradshaw
  James, 111
Brazoria, 125, 239
Brazoria Bar, 224
Brazos River, 13, 41, 123, 143
Brazos Valley-Houston, 268
Broocks
  Travis G., 168, 183
Brooke
  John C., 183
Brown
  Dr. Lemuel B., 242
  John, 274
Brownsville, 277
Bucarelli
  Viceroy Antonio, 24
Buena Vista, 278
Buffalo Bayou, 143
Bullock
  James Whitis, 111
Burditt
  Jesse, 180

burial ground
  Protestant, 153
  Roman Catholic, 153
Burleson
  Edward, 139, 160
Burnet
  David G., 149
Burroughs
  James M., 272, 274
Burton
  Isaac W., 111
Butler
  George, 127

-C-

Canada, 127
Canfield
  A. W., 269
Capers
  Bishop, 183
Carizzo Creek, 105
Carrol
  General William, 57
Carthage, 209(2)
Cartwright
  John, 180
Catholic Church, 212
Cavalier
  Robert, Sieur de La Salle, 9
Cedars
  Jack, 118
Center, 117, 210
Chaplin
  Chichester, 77, 83, 105
Cherokee War, 72,

307

Cherokee War
  (continued)
  (continued)
Chihuahua, 43
Chireno
  Encarnacion, 90,
  114
Chonca
  Christobal, 56
Christian Church,
  210
Civil War, 185, 206,
  210, 275
Clarksville, 211,
  233, 268
Coahuila, 15, 241
Coleto Creek, 142
Collinsworth
  Captain George,
  139
Colorado River, 123
Columbia, 149
Columbia District,
  136, 137
Constitution of
  1824, 111, 155,
  188
Consultation of
  1832, 114, 131,
  234
Consultation of
  1833, 114
Consultation of
  1835, 114, 158,
  208
Convention of 1832,
  126, 145
Convention of 1833,
  126, 131, 136
Convention of 1836,
  114, 138, 143,
  232, 234
Convention of 1845,
  232, 233
Convention of 1866,
  236
Convention of 1875,
  236
Cordova
  Vicente, 111,
  154, 156, 159
Cordovan Rebellion,
  153, 157, 194,
  232
Corpus Christi, 277
Corzine
  Shelby, 157, 232
Council Creek, 160
County
  Anderson, 152,
  162, 209
  Angelina, 127,
  152
  Bowie, 210
  Camp, 152
  Cherokee, 3, 118,
  152, 155
  Dallas, 152
  Delta, 152
  Gregg, 152
  Harrison, 116,
  162, 166, 209,
  274
  Henderson, 152,
  161, 162, 235
  Hill, 41
  Hopkins, 152
  Houston, 152,
  162, 165, 175,
  232, 274
  Jasper, 99, 232,
  274

Jefferson, 232
Kaufman, 152, 235
Liberty, 61
Limestone, 43
Madison, 25
Marion, 116
McLennan, 41
Montgomery, 127, 209
Nacogdoches, 3, 13, 97, 152, 156, 168, 176, 205(2), 209, 211, 231, 232, 233, 234, 243, 267, 272, 274, 278
Newton, 99
Panola, 99, 116
Raines, 152
Red River, 197, 211, 233, 268
Rockwall, 152
Rusk, 3, 14, 116, 152, 162, 168
Sabine, 3, 93, 96, 99, 118, 119, 162, 168, 171, 198, 204, 205, 208, 209, 232, 243, 258, 267, 272, 274
San Augustine, 3, 56, 89, 93, 96, 99, 127, 140, 162, 166, 168, 200, 205, 208, 210, 232, 233, 234(2), 243, 272, 274(2)
Shelby, 3, 93, 96, 99, 116, 156, 162, 166(2), 171, 190, 195, 204, 210, 232, 234, 243, 258, 267, 272, 274
Smith, 3, 152
Trinity, 152
Tyler, 121, 129
Upshur, 116, 152
Van Zandt, 3, 152, 161
Washington, 206
Wood, 152
County Court, 225, 228, 229, 230
Cow Creek, 200
Cravens
  James M., 165, 166
Crawford
  William C., 141, 142
Crockett, 165, 175
Cumberland
  Presbyterian Church, 196, 204
  Sunday School, 206
Cumberland River, 118
Cunningham
  Andrew J., 180

-D-

D'Spain
  Lynn, 211
Daggett
  Ephriam M., 236

Darnell
  Nicholas H., 272, 273
Davenport
  Juan Bernardo, 77
  Samuel, 4, 33, 36, 46, 49, 59, 68, 77
Davis
  Alexander M., 183
  Nathan, 99, 116
Defee
  Dr. William, 211
Department of Bexar, 78(2), 115
  Political Chief, 78
Department of Nacogdoches, 115, 151, 189, 219
Department of the Brazos, 219
  Political Chief, 138
DeWitt
  Green, 139
Dill Creek, 14
District Courts of Texas, 225, 227, 228
Douglass, 156
  Kelsey H., 160, 169, 203
Durst
  John, 113, 114, 155
  Joseph, 87
Durst's Ferry, 113
Dwire, 206

-E-

East Hamilton, 267
Echols
  William F., 274
Edwards
  Asa N., 114
  Benjamin, 84, 88, 102
  Benjamin Wroe, 84
  Elizabeth Turner, 77
  Haden, 65, 75, 79, 81, 84(2), 91, 102, 203
  Haden H., 274
  Haden Harrison, 77
  Jane, 77
  John, 76
  Susan Wroe, 77
  Susannah Beall, 77
  Susannah Wroe, 76
  Tabitha Beall, 77, 83
  William C., 274
Eight Mile Baptist Church, 209
El Mexico, 269
England, 126
  London, 72
English
  George, 99
  James, 226
  John, 130
  William, 127

-F-

Fannin

Colonel James W., 142
Father of Nacogdoches, 21
Fields
  Richard, 71, 88, 89
Filsola
  General Vicente, 154
Fisher
  George, 123
Fitzallen
  O., 183
Flat Fork Creek, 167
Flores
  Gil, 24, 25
Florida, 141
Foote
  Henry S., 47
Forbes
  John, 145, 158, 226, 242
Fort Houston, 209
Fort Jessup, 119
Fort Teran, 121
Fowler
  Littleton, 200
  Reverend
    Littleton, 183
Foye
  Frederick, 127, 128
France, 233
Fredericksburg, 239
Fredonian Rebellion, 65, 77, 87, 100, 102, 128
French West Indies, 37
Fullerton's Landing, 267

-G-

Gaceta de Texas, 269
Gaines
  General Edmund P., 118
  General Edward Pendleton, 51
  James, 51, 66, 118, 119
  James T., 141, 142
Gaines Ferry, 119
Galveston, 60, 62, 106, 275
Galveston Bay, 123
Galvez
  Count de, 9
Garrett
  Jacob, 99, 127, 128, 135
Garzo
  Dr. Jayme, 241
Gates
  Brother G., 210
Gateway to Texas, 101
Geneva (Shawnee Village), 119
George
  Alfred, 163, 164
Georgia, 69, 93, 124, 128, 141, 148, 279
Germany, 102, 126
  Cologne, 130
  Hanover, 242
Goliad, 139, 194, 239, 249

Gonzales, 139
Goodbread
  Joseph, 163, 164
Goodman Bridge, 13
Gould
  Charles, 203
Goyens
  William, 115
Grant
  James, 142
Grayson
  Peter W., 132
Great Britain, 233
Guadalupe River, 52, 139
Gulf of Mexico, 60, 79, 91, 151, 265, 275

-H-

Hall
  James, 165
  Samuel N., 165
Hamilton
  Andrew S., 204
Hangman's Hill, 208
Hanks
  Wyatt, 111, 127
Hansford
  John M., 164
Harrisburg, 143
Harrison
  Jonas, 128, 132
  William Henry, 84
Hastings
  Thomas, 126, 130
Henderson
  Frances C., 207
  James Pinckney, 183, 207, 224, 259, 272, 273, 274
Hernandez
  Juana Luzgarda, 21
Herrin
  Lemuel, 209
Hertz
  Dr. John, 242
  Dr. Joseph, 242
  Hyman, 126
Hickman's Prairie, 210
Hicks
  Archibald W. O., 234, 272
Hidalgo
  Father, 13
Hilliard's Spring, 167
Hinds
  Joseph, 207
Hoffman
  David, 135
Hogg
  Joseph L., 272
Holloway
  Lewis, 56
Holman
  William W., 180
Holt
  Benjamin, 126
Hopewell, 209
Horton
  Alexander, 99, 135, 168
Hotchkiss
  Augustus, 180
Houston, 143, 178, 254, 275
  Sam, 72, 114,

130, 132, 138,
143, 149, 155,
158, 168, 190,
250, 274
Hungary, 123
Hunter
  John Dunn, 71,
    88, 89
Huston
  Almanson, 135,
    180

-I-

Illinois, 209
Independence, 206
Indiana
  Hamilton County,
    138
Indians
  Alabama, 120, 161
  Biloxi, 156
  Caddo, 3, 7, 19,
    22, 28, 68, 100
  Caddo (Hasinai),
    13
  Caddos (Nazoni
    and Nadaco), 14
  Cherokee, 3, 72,
    88, 120
  Cherokees, 69,
    71, 76, 89, 94,
    132, 146, 155,
    156, 159, 161
  Chickasaw, 206
  Choctaws, 147
  Comanche, 25, 40
  Coshatta, 121,
    161
  Creek Nation, 147
  Iones, 156

  Kickapoos, 159
  Seminoles, 147
  Shawnees, 159,
    161
  Tejas, 13
  Tonkawas, 94
  Waco, 94
Ireland, 83
  Belfast, 40
  Londonderry,
    Ulster County,
    33
  Navare, 34
Irion
  Dr. Robert
    Anderson, 244
Ironosa Creek, 96
Isaacs
  Elijah, 128

-J-

Jack
  Patrick, 110,
    124, 125
  Spencer H., 132
  William H., 125
Jackson
  Charles W., 164
  General Andrew,
    44, 58
Jasper, 265
Jefferson
  Thomas, 69
Johnson
  Archilles Edmund
    Challis, 131,
    135
  Frank W., 142
  James B., 170
Johnston

Johnston (continued)
  Albert S., 159
Jones
  Anson, 272, 273
  William, 87
Jonesborough (Pecan
  Point), 197, 199
Journal and
  Advertiser, 269
Justice Courts, 225
Justice of the
  Peace, 229, 230

-K-

Kaufman
  David S., 168,
  204, 274
Kellog
  Albert G., 135,
  180
Kendall
  Henry, 182
Kentucky, 40, 44,
  49, 84, 86, 93,
  123, 127, 131,
  148, 197, 279,
  207
  Bowling Green,
    201
  Caldwell County,
    201
  Christian County,
    141
  Frankfort, 41
  Indiana County,
    127
  Louisville, 201
  Paris, Bourbon
    County, 76
  Transylvania
    College, 244
Kentucky Annual
  Confreence, 201
Kingdom of New
  Spain, 18
Korn
  Dr. Jesse, 242

-L-

La Bahia (Goliad),
  52, 62
La Bahia Presidio,
  240
La Nana Creek, 7,
  26, 65, 100, 257
Labadie
  Dr. Nicholas
  Descomp, 242
Laffite
  Jean, 60
LaGrange College,
  201
Lamar
  M. B., 149, 157,
  159, 190
Landrum
  Colonel Willis
  H., 156, 160
Lara
  Bernardo
  Gutierrez de,
  46, 47, 49, 52,
  59
Las Boreagas, 120
Le Moyne
  Pierre, Sieur
  d'Iberville, 12
LeGrand
  Edwin, 140
  Edwin O., 234

Liberty, 121, 124
Liberty District, 137
Little Cow Creek, 99
Long
  Dr. James, 57
  James, 60, 62
Long Expeditions, 47, 57, 119
Loony
  James, 128
  Samuel, 128
Los Adaes, 15, 17, 20(2), 23, 26, 93
Los Ais, 20, 22
Louisiana, 4, 30, 86, 131, 135, 164, 197, 198, 264, 279
  Fort Jessup, 46
  Logansport, 204
  Natchitoches, 16, 18, 21, 23, 28, 33, 36, 46, 47, 49, 51, 54, 58, 62, 119, 175, 192, 265, 269
  Neutral Ground, 34, 36, 46, 48, 50, 162
  Neutral Strip, 79, 119
  New Orleans, 9, 23, 37, 40, 44, 49, 55, 62, 114, 136, 265, 268
  Rapides Parish, 197
  Robeline, 14
  Sabine Parish, 207
  Shreveport, 265
Louisiana Territory, 20, 37(2), 68
Love
  John G., 183, 226
Lovell
  F. G., 183

-M-

Mabitt
  Captain L. H., 168
Macedonia Baptist Church, 209
Madero
  Francisco, 124
Magee
  Augustus, 46, 47, 49, 52, 119
Magee-Gutierrez Expedition, 46, 55, 59, 61, 119
Makemie
  Rev. John, 206
Margil
  Father Antonio de Jesus, 14
Maryland
  St. Mary's County, 66
Masonic Order
  Redland Lodge No. 3, 185
Massachusetts, 46
  Auburn, 198
Massanet
  Father, 10
Matagorda, 106
Matthews

Matthews (continued)
  Mansil W., 211
Mayo
  Herman B., 77, 87
  John W., 87
McDonald
  Donald, 127
McFarland
  Thomas S., 105
  William, 127,
    132, 180, 234
McKinney
  Collin, 210
McMahan
  James B., 199
  Samuel B., 199
McMahan settlement,
  201
McMahan's Camp
  Ground, 202
McMahan's Chapel,
  200, 202
Menard District, 121
Menchaca
  Antonio, 155, 157
  Captain Jose
    Alferez Miguel,
    48
Merchant
  Edward, 165
Methodist Annual
  Conference, 184
Methodist Board of
  Missions, 200
Methodist Church,
  181, 182, 196,
  197, 199, 200,
  203, 207, 212
Methodist Episcopal
  Church, 201
Mexican Advocate,
  269
Mexican Constitution
  of 1824, 140
Mexican Revolution,
  68, 74, 257
Mexican War, 168,
  236
Mexican War
  (1846-1848), 191
Mexico, 137, 140,
  152, 157
Mexico City, 18, 24,
  27, 63, 67, 80,
  88, 104, 114,
  132
Mier y Teran
  Manuel de, 102
Migelson
  Dr. Joseph, 242
Milam, 171, 198, 204
  Ben, 120, 139
  Benjamin Rush, 62
Milam settlement,
  119
Mill Creek, 13
Millard
  Henry, 137
  Mrs. Massie, 209
Mission Hill, 92
Mission La Purisima
  Conception, 16
Mission Nuestra
  Senora de
  Guadalupe
  de los
    Nacogdoches, 13,
  16
Mission Nuestra
  Senora de la
  Purisma
  Conception de los

Hainai, 13
Mission Nuestra Senora de los Ais, 92
Mission Nuestra Senora de los Delores de los Ais, 14, 16
Mission Nuestro Padre San Francisco de los Tejas, 13
Mission Nuestro Senor San Jose de los Nazonis, 14
Mission San Francisco de los Neches, 16, 117
Mission San Francisco de los Tejas, 10, 187
Mission San Jose de los Nazonis, 16
Mission San Miguel de Linares de los Adaes, 14, 16
Mission Santisimo Nombre de Maria, 10
Mississippi, 34, 86, 93, 137, 165, 211, 279, 206
  Hinds County, 75
  Jackson, Hinds County, 84
  Natchez, 41, 42, 57, 58, 66
  Pearl River, 72, 77
  Pike County, 129
  Port Gibson, 58
Mississippi Annual Conference, 197, 200, 201
Mississippi River, 57, 69, 119
Missouri, 66, 131, 207, 279, 207
  St. Charles, 197
Moderator-Regulator feud, 236
Moderators, 165, 167
Monroe
  James, 49
Monterey, 278
Montrose
  Reverend Marcus A., 181, 182
Moore
  Colonel J. H., 139
  Elder, 210
Moorman
  Charles W., 165, 166
Mora
  Estevan, 157
  Juan de la, 25
Morrell
  Z. N., 208
Mott
  James, 226
Moz
  Frederick, 111
Muckleroy
  David, 274, 278
Muncipality
  Teneha, 141
Municipality

Municipality
  (continued)
  Jasper, 151
  Jefferson, 151
  Liberty, 121, 151
  Nacogdoches, 78,
    96, 100, 117,
    118, 120,
    130(2), 135,
    140, 231, 242
  Sabine, 118, 141,
    151
  San Augustine,
    95, 98, 99, 104,
    118, 135, 141,
    151, 199, 208,
    235, 242
  Shelby, 116, 141,
    151
  Tenehaw, 116
Murphy
  Edward, 4, 33(2)
Mustang Prairie, 209
Myrick's Ferry, 204

-N-

Nacogdoches, 3, 7,
    13, 19, 20, 28,
    29, 34, 36, 40,
    45, 50, 56, 58,
    60(2), 65, 75,
    81, 82, 93, 101,
    111, 119, 125,
    126, 131, 133,
    150, 154, 157,
    169, 174, 178,
    179, 185, 188,
    192, 198, 203,
    206, 209, 226,
    239, 254, 255,
    260, 264, 270,
    261, 271, 269,
    208
  Ayuntimento, 147
  Church Plaza,
    101, 112
  Church Square,
    193
  County
    Courthouse, 193
  Gateway to Texas,
    33
  Guadalupe
    Mission, 192
  Masonic Hall, 207
  North Street, 112
  Plaza Principal,
    28, 101, 186
  The Protestant
    Elm, 197
  Washington
    Square, 187
Nacogdoches County,
  209
Nacogdoches
  District, 3, 31,
  91, 126, 130
Nacogdoches News,
  269
Nacogdoches
  University, 185
Nacogdoches-San
  Augustine area,
  210
Nacogdoches-San
  Augustine
  District, 66
Nashville
  (Shelbyville),
  116(2)
National Militia,

INDEX

Navasota River, 79
Neches District, 129
Neches River, 3, 10, 13, 16, 118, 120, 161
Neches settlement, 111
Neustra Senora del Pilar de Nacogdoches, 26
New Bethel Church, 209
New Braunfels, 239
New England, 31
New Hope, 208
New Jersey, 242
  Woodbridge Township, 128
New Mexico, 45
New Orleans Grays, 130
New Phillipines, 15
New Spain, 41
New York, 34, 72, 126, 269
Noble
  James M., 274
Nolan
  Philip, 39
Norris
  Samuel, 66, 84(2), 102, 119
  Susanna, 119
North Carolina, 72, 115, 127, 129, 136, 140, 207
  Bethany, 206
  Fayetteville, 141
  Granville, 140
  Halifax County, 136
Nueces River, 277
Nuevo Santander, 47

-O-

O'connor
  Hugo, 23
Ochiltree
  William B., 168, 224, 233, 272, 274
Ohio, 243
Ohio River, 118
Oklahoma, 160
Old North Baptist Church, 209
Old South, 79, 81, 117
Old Southwest, 70
Old Southwest Territory, 56
Old Three hundred, 128
Order of the Eastern Star, 185
Orton Hill, 51

-P-

Padilla
  Juan Antonio, 109
  Maria Davila, 22
Palestine, 209
Palo Alto, 277
Palo Gaucho, 96
Palo Gaucho Bayou, 56
Panola County, 209
Parker
  Daniel, 135, 208

Parker (continued)
  Isaac, 274
  Jesse, 126
Parmer
  Emily, 83
  Martin, 66, 83, 87, 90, 102, 140, 142
Paso Tomas, 25
Patonia, 267
Patroon Creek, 96
Pennington
  Sydney O., 141
Pennsylvania, 34
  Carlisle, Cumberland County, 34
  Lancaster, 127
  Philadelphia, 33
  Pittsburg, 33
Peres
  Jose Antonio, 157
Perkins
  James, 183
Piedras
  Colonel Jose de las, 102, 109, 111, 113, 125
Pike
  General Zebulon, 45
Pine Hill, 111
Poe
  Reverend Daniel, 183
Polk
  James K., 273
Ponton
  Andrew, 139
Potter
  Robert, 140, 142

Presbyterian Church, 181, 196, 212
Presbyterian Church (U. S. A.), 206
Presbyterian Synod, 205
Presidio Dolores de los Tejas, 17
Presidio Nuestra Senora de los Dolores de los Tejas, 13
Presidio Nuestra Senora del Pilar, 16
Princeton University, 206
Prison of the Inquisition, 132
Procela
  Luis, 82
Procella
  Jose, 157
Protestant Episcopal Church, 207, 212
  Committee on Domestic Missions, 207
Province of Alsace Strassburg, 241
Provisional Government, 225, 208
  General Council, 128, 145
  Lieutenant Governor, 138
  President, 145

-Q-

INDEX

Quinalty
  John, 4
Quirk
  Edmund, 56, 105
  Edmund
    (Raymundo), 4

-R-

Raguet
  Henry, 169
Raines
  Emory, 226, 272
Ramon
  Captain Domingo, 12, 14
Rancho El Lobanillo, 21, 22
Ratcliff
  William D., 183
Reagan
  John H., 235
Red House, 112, 186
Red Lands, 92, 95, 105, 118, 144
Red Mound, 120
Red River, 18, 59(2), 88, 154, 201
Red River Circuit, 201
Redlander, 182, 269, 270
Reed
  Isaac, 209
Refugio, 194
Regulator-Moderator Feud, 162
Regulator-Moderator War, 117
Regulators, 66, 86, 164, 166
Republic of Fredonia, 88
Republic of Mexico, 68, 97, 277, 278
Republic of Texas, 78, 142, 144, 148, 149, 151, 155, 159, 169, 170, 172, 173, 178, 183, 184, 212, 213, 220, 226, 230, 234, 245, 251, 262, 270, 208
Constitution, 190
Republican Army of the North, 49, 54, 55
Resaca de la Palma, 277
Rey
  Yldefonso, 240
Ring Tailed Panther, 67
Rio Bravo (Rio Grande), 28
Rio Grande, 47, 54, 88, 107, 144, 277
Rios
  Domingo Teran de los, 92, 93
Ripperda
  Governor, 24
Rivera
  General Pedro de, 17(2)
Roads
  El Camino del Caballo, 175

Roads (continued)
  El Camino Real,
    28, 65, 96, 101,
    118, 120, 175,
    264
  John Durst, 113
  King's Highway,
    94, 96, 105,
    119, 135, 136,
    175, 193
  La Bahia
    (Goliad), 25
  Old San Antonio,
    28, 92, 118, 275
  Old Spanish
    Trail, 121
  Royal, 3, 22(2),
    25, 26, 65, 101
  San Antonio, 264
  San
    Antonio-Nacogdoches, 28, 88
  Smugglers' Road,
    175
  Smugglers' Trace,
    175
Roark
  Amos, 205
Robbins
  Nathan, 135
Roberts
  Elisha, 99, 127,
    131, 180
  John S., 67, 87,
    90, 120, 140.,
    169
Robinson
  James W., 135,
    138
  Jesse J., 274
Roman Catholic
  Church, 193
Ross
  Reuben, 53
Rowe
  Dr. Joseph, 180
Runaway Scrape, 143,
  148
Runnells
  Henry A., 165
Rusk
  Thomas J., 135,
    140, 142, 155,
    156, 159, 169,
    186, 203, 224,
    231, 272, 160,
    273, 274
Russell
  Reverend James,
    182
Ruter
  Dr. Martin, 200

-S-

Sabine, 111, 192
Sabine Baptist
  Association, 210
Sabine District,
  127, 130
Sabine Pass, 267
Sabine River, 3, 22,
  28, 34, 37, 41,
  45, 50, 51, 55,
  56, 58, 65, 68,
  70, 76, 78, 91,
  93, 97, 99, 116,
  119, 147, 162,
  196, 197, 200,
  202, 204, 207,
  265(2), 267, 275
Sabinetown, 120, 267

INDEX

Saltillo, 47, 80, 86, 132
San Antonio Bar, 224
San Antonio de Bexar, 3, 14, 15, 20, 23, 25, 27, 31, 36, 43, 45, 52, 54, 60, 63, 78, 84, 86, 94, 107, 111, 114(2), 117, 133, 139, 175, 187, 194, 198, 241, 264, 278
San Antonio River, 18, 23
San Augustine, 3, 14, 22, 28, 92, 111, 135, 136, 147, 154, 156, 157, 167, 170, 174, 178, 179, 187, 189, 192, 195, 201, 204, 205, 207, 211, 224, 226, 232, 235, 239, 255, 258, 259, 265, 269, 270
  Masonic Hall, 208
  Mission Dolores, 192
  townsite, 131
San Augustine Bar, 224
San Augustine Circuit, 201
San Augustine District, 127, 130, 138, 193
San Augustine University, 179, 182
San Augustine-Nacogdoches district, 268
San Felipe, 79, 88, 111, 125, 130, 133, 143, 242
San Jacinto, 249
San Jacinto River, 124, 143
San Juan Bautista, 12
San Luis Potosi, 43
San Patricio, 194
San Pedro River, 54
Sanchez
  Father Benito, 14
Sanson
  Henry, 207
Santa Anna
  General Antonio L., 111, 125, 134, 137, 142, 144
Scotland, 71
Scurry
  Richardson A., 233
Secession Convention of 1861, 235
Seiger
  W. N., 226
Sepulveda
  Jose Antonio, 66, 82, 87
Seven Years' War, 23
Shaler
  William, 49
Shelbyville, 141,

Shelbyville
  (continued)
    (continued)
Siege of Bexar, 140
Sigler
  William N., 135
Simms
  Charles H., 126,
    169
Smith
  Dr. Ashbel, 245
  George W., 226
  Gilbert M. L.,
    186
  Henry, 138(2)
  Luther, 33
  Mary, 186
  Mitchell, 205
Solis
  Father Jose
    Gaspar De, 20
South Carolina, 124,
    196
  Pendleton
    District, 231,
    209
  Spartanburg, 71
Spain, 233
Spangerberg
  Dr. Agustin
    Guillermo de,
    241
Spanish Bluff
  (Trinidad), 51
Spanish Bluff
  Crossing, 176
Sparks
  William, 203
Sprowl
  John, 99
St. Denis

Louis Juchereau
  de, 12, 16, 93,
  118
Starr
  Dr. James Harper,
    243
  James H., 169,
    186
State of Coahuila y
  Texas, 74, 78,
  129, 170, 178,
  188, 218
State of Cohuila y
  Texas, 131
State of Texas, 214
Stephenson
  Henry, 197, 200
Sterne
  Adolphus, 102,
  130, 169
Stevenson
  James P., 198
  William, 196, 198
Stivers
  Dr. Samuel, 242
Stone House, 102,
  112
Stone House (Old
  Stone Fort), 27,
  88, 257
Strickland
  James, 164
Sublett
  Henry W., 274
  Phillip A., 127,
  131, 180
Sullivan
  P. F., 210
Sunday Schools, 203
Supreme Court
  State of Texas,

INDEX

233
Supreme Court of
  Texas, 226
  Chief Justice,
    224

-T-

Taylor
  Charles S., 126,
    131, 140, 186,
    234, 272
  General Zachary,
    277
Teal
  George, 180, 200
Tehuacana Hill, 43
Tenaha (Shelby)
  District, 130
Tenaha (Teneja,
  Tenaha, Teneha)
  District, 116
Tenahaw District, 96
Teneha, 111
Teneha (Shelby), 226
Tenehaw (Shelby)
  District, 128
Tennessee, 49, 69,
  86, 93, 116,
  128, 148, 196,
  211, 279
  Benton County,
    209
  Maury County, 57
  Murfreesboro, 205
  Nashville, 51,
    118, 131, 136
  Smith County,
    198, 200
Tennessee Annual
  Conference, 196,
    200
Tennessee Cumberland
  Presbytery, 198
Terrell
  George W., 224,
    232
Texas Annual
  Conference, 202
Texas Revolution,
  114, 130, 154,
  170, 199, 204,
  209, 237, 277,
  244
The Texas Chronicle,
  269
The Texas
  Republican, 269
Thomas
  Iredell D., 180
Thompson
  Burrell J., 87
Thorn
  Frost, 77, 169,
    186, 203
Town Bluff, 121
Travis
  William B., 110,
    124, 125
Trinity River, 15,
  25(2), 41, 51,
  61, 70, 78, 94,
  115, 151, 175,
  232
Truitt
  James, 274
Two Seed Baptist
  Church, 209
Tyler, 161

-U-

University of East
    Texas, 184
University of
    Edinburg, 181,
    182
Urrea
    General Jose, 142

-V-

Van Zandt
    Issac, 168
Velasco, 114, 125
Vergara
    Father Gabriel,
    13
Village de San
    Fernando, 24
Virginia, 31, 118,
    130, 136, 197,
    208
    Culpeper, 51
    Culpeper County,
    57
    New River, 128
    Stafford County,
    75

-W-

Waco, 43
Walker
    Richard S., 274
    W. W., 58
Wallace
    Benjamin R., 274
War of 1812, 55, 58,
    67, 84, 127
Washington, D. C.,
    47
Washington-on-the-Br

azos, 114, 134,
    140, 143, 201,
    208, 264, 265
Watkins
    Richard O., 205,
    206
Watkins Settlement
    Presbyterian
    Church, 205
Wesleyan College,
    183
Wharton
    John A., 136, 137
Wheeler
    Royal T., 224,
    233
Whitaker
    William, 135
Whitcomb
    Dr. Joseph, 242
White River, 69
Wilkinson
    General James,
    40, 46, 58
    Jane Herbert, 58
Wilson
    Reverend Francis,
    182
    Reverend Hugh,
    206
Wolf Creek, 209
Woll
    General Adrian,
    157
Woodville, 121
Writing Schools, 190

-Y-

Y'Barbo
    Antonio Gil, 21,

22, 25, 27, 30, 92, 174, 193, 257
Matheo Antonio, 21
Ysletta Creek, 115

-Z-

Zervan
  Dr. Federico, 241

www.ingramcontent.com/pod-product-compliance
Lightning Source LLC
Chambersburg PA
CBHW071315150426
43191CB00007B/625